BEST OF THE BEST PRESENTS

THE CROWN
OF SOUTHERN COOKING

*Recipes from the
Birthplace of the Blues*

Evelyn Roughton

QUAIL RIDGE PRESS
Preserving America's Food Heritage

To my precious Tony, Jennifer, Kevin, and Wanda, and everyone in our extended family who for generations has been great cooks and thankful guests at wonderful shared meals. We love cooking together and eating together; the more the merrier around our tables! The *Best of the Best* family has also been such a blessing, and I thank them for making my family a part of theirs.

Library of Congress Cataloging-in-Publication Data

Roughton, Evelyn.
 The crown of southern cooking : recipes from the birthplace of the blues
/ by Evelyn Roughton.
    pages cm
 Includes index.
 ISBN 978-1-938879-15-9
 1. Cooking, American--Southern style. I. Title.
 TX715.2.S68.R68 2015
 641.5975--dc23   2015019513

ISBN 978-1-938879-15-9

Manufactured in the United States of America
First printing, August 2015

On the front cover: The Crown's Pavlova, page 198
On the back cover: The Crown's Chicken Allison, page 114, and Black Butter Green Beans, page 86.
All photos by Jennifer Schaumburg, except: Wanda Adams: pages 54, 57, 149, 162, 173, 195;
Tom Beetz: page 10, www.flickr.com/photos/9967007@N07/6577873073; Jack Catlette: page 21;
Deanna Contrino: pages 180, 181; Beth MacLeod: back cover, pages 48, 71, 115, 119, 131, 218;
Gwen McKee: pages 24, 42, 50, 68, 89, 110, 165, 167, 170; Roy Meek: pages 6, 79, 116; Jim Steeby: page 64

QUAIL RIDGE PRESS
P. O. Box 123 • Brandon, MS 39043 • 1-800-343-1583
info@quailridge.com • www.quailridge.com

CONTENTS

PREFACE

The Crown Restaurant opened in 1976, inside our antique shop, situated in the cotton fields of the Mississippi Delta. We only served lunch, because if we opened at night, we wouldn't have the time we wanted for our family, and it would actually feel like work. Now, nearly forty years later, we still serve only lunch, with pie and coffee all day, and it still doesn't feel like work—we love every minute!

When lunch guests arrive, we feel we are welcoming friends—ones we've known for years, and brand-new friends visiting Indianola for the first time. We want them all to feel at home at The Crown. That's our mission: to make sure our guests enjoy their meals, experience real southern hospitality, and leave The Crown as "old friends."

The Crown has hosted thousands of "blues pilgrims" from across the world, arriving in tour buses and in cars, who are here expressly to visit the B.B. King Museum and Delta Interpretive Center, and to just soak up the atmosphere of the Mississippi Delta, the true "Birthplace of the Blues." In just one week this spring, we had guests from France, British Colombia, Japan, Norway, Australia, and all over the United States. The world loves the blues, and B.B. King, and our little town of Indianola, which is the heart of the Delta!

When my sister Wanda, Mama, and I opened The Crown, my husband Tony built it as a replica of a pub or tearoom, much like the ones we loved in England. Guests were served on antique tables and chairs with everything for sale, even the dessert cart that was pushed from table to table. And yes, we sold lots of tea carts over the years. The desserts are now on a table for guests to help themselves, and they enjoy having a sliver of each of the pies and some Pavlova and trifle with their coffee after lunch. We still serve on antiques, and they are all for sale, with local art and pottery filling the dining room and gift shop, along with our Taste of Gourmet line of packaged mixes and condiments that were created from The Crown's recipes and our love of food.

Tony and I lived in Thailand for a year and in England for four years while he was in the Air Force. We traveled extensively, eating exotic foods, and tasting everything we came across on our adventures. We talked a lot about opening a restaurant someday, serving the luscious foods we so enjoyed.

When we left the Air Force, we came home to Indianola, and The Crown was born in a steel-frame building filled with the English antiques we had been importing since 1972. The atmosphere was different, the food was unique to the area, but before long, it seemed like the entire Mississippi Delta came to our cotton field to enjoy a "day away" from the ordinary. We did lots of special events in the evenings—rehearsal parties, corporate dinners, afternoon teas, wedding brunches, and lots of catering events, and we made each event a little "different"—an occasion of its own.

Tony and Evelyn Roughton at The Crown

When the catfish industry was growing in the Delta, we took on another mission—to prove that our local catfish could be cooked like any other firm white fish, and it did *not* have to be fried. In 1987, we created our delicious Smoked Catfish Paté that won the 1990 International Fancy Food Award for Best Hors d'Oeuvre in New York. Serving our local catfish with French and Asian sauces led to our first cookbook, *Classic Catfish*, in 1992. It included a lot of southern favorites using our local catfish, instead of shrimp, crab, or redfish. The media came, too, because of the catfish, the blues heritage, and our unique, good food. CNN, Bobby Flay with his *Food Nation*, Turner South's *Blue Ribbon* show, and the Travel Channel have all filmed live in my kitchen, and there have been articles in *Cooks Magazine, Southern Living, Bon Appétit, Saveur, Country Living*, and so many others. We have been truly blessed!

The Crown and Taste of Gourmet is a family business and always has been, since Mama and Wanda and I cooked the first meal in March of 1976. Our children Jennifer and Kevin grew up in The Crown, doing all sorts of jobs, including serving desserts and delivering antique furniture, and Kevin even illustrated our *Classic*

Catfish cookbook. Jennifer has been our designer of catalogs, packaging, and promotions for years, and is now in charge of The Crown...and she is there every day. Grandchildren Sage and Prescott run the cash register, help serve bread in the dining room, and work with us at the plant after school and during holidays.

Tony and I are at The Crown every day during lunch to visit with guests. My own joy is to pass the bread, insisting that "we don't want you to go away hungry." Of course, it's

Artisan pottery available in The Crown's gift shop

also a great way to visit with everyone, find out where they are from, where they are going, and if we can help them find one of the back roads— those out-of-the-way places that make the Mississippi Delta so unique. And we do know some back roads!

Jennifer arranges a display of locally made products

The Crown is the ultimate family business, and we have received so much pleasure from every aspect of it. We love the people of the Delta who have lunched and shopped with us for more than forty years, and we love sharing our Delta with the blues and heritage tourists who are coming in droves. Our customers have become friends we will treasure forever. In that simple fact lies the pure joy of this business. We have been blessed, and we give praise and thanks to God, who gave us these friends, our family, and all of our many, many blessings.

Evelyn Roughton

B.B. KING

"The Thrill is Gone"...
but B.B. King's music, his smile, and his love will live forever.

From the cotton fields, street corners, and juke joints of the Mississippi Delta came a new kind of music—the blues. Considered by most to be the only truly indigenous American music, this form that has influenced musicians worldwide is deeply rooted in

B.B. King, "King of the Blues"

Delta soil. And so is the man who helped spread the blues as its foremost ambassador—Riley B. King. He proudly introduced himself at concerts across the world, "I'm from Indianola, Mississippi," and his hometown loves him.

B.B. King played everywhere... for sophisticated blues fans in Europe, poor people in Mississippi, the Pope at the Vatican, and thousands upon thousands during a six-decade touring career. Riley B. King (September 16, 1925–May 14, 2015), known by his stage name B.B. King, opened for the Rolling Stones in 1969, and won the first of his 15 Grammys in 1970 for "The Thrill is Gone." B.B. was inducted into the American Blues Hall of Fame in 1980, received the Kennedy Center Honors in 1995, the Presidential Medal of Freedom in 2006 from President George W. Bush, and in 2012 sang "Sweet Home Chicago" in the White House with President Barack Obama.

King was also known for performing tirelessly throughout his musical career, appearing at more than 200 concerts per year well into his 70s. With his guitar "Lucille" strapped to his chest, he performed and recorded decades of musical hits, recording with U2 in 1988, "When Love Comes to Town," and in 2000, an album with Eric Clapton that sold more than 2 million, "Riding with the King," B.B.'s best-selling album.

B.B. King never forgot his roots, and for 35 years, he and his band returned to his hometown of Indianola to give an outdoor concert, the B.B. King Homecoming

Concert at Fletcher Park, so the children and people of Indianola could hear them play—and they never charged a fee. On May 25, 2014, at the last B.B. King Homecoming Concert, the King of the Blues, at 88, played for more than an hour to a packed crowd outside the museum. On May 30, 2015, he was laid to rest on the grounds of his museum. Indianola will continue the B.B. King Homecoming in his honor on the first Saturday in June each year at Fletcher Park.

Indianola, a small Delta town of 11,000, opened the $16 million B.B. King Museum and Delta Interpretive Center in 2008, dedicated to celebrating the life and music of this iconic artist. It was B.B.'s expressed wish that education and community outreach be at the heart of the museum's mission. The museum honors him and his legacy by providing educational programs designed to offer young people the kind of hope and opportunity that was not available to Riley B. King in the Mississippi of his youth. The stories of the Delta—its history, music, social customs, race relations, literature and legends, adversities and successes—are synthesized in one interpretive setting. All these elements came together to produce the men and women who created blues music, and the B.B. King Museum and Delta Interpretive Center serves as a repository for the rich heritage that gave birth to America's music.

B.B. King died at the age of 89 on May 14, 2015. People lined the streets when his funeral procession passed through the Delta and into Indianola. Five thousand paid their respects as he lay in state at the museum. He will be greatly missed by his friends, his family, his hometown, and his multitudes of fans worldwide. His legacy will never be forgotten, and his "Thrill" will never be gone.

B.B. King Museum and Delta Interpretive Center

APPETIZERS & BEVERAGES

Janice's Hot Crawfish Dip

DILL DIP IN A BREAD BOWL

MAKES 2 CUPS.

Wonderful with crackers or chips, and as a dip for fresh vegetables. The bread bowl is always fun for small casual parties. For more elegant affairs (when everyone is dressed up) or cocktail buffets, I like to serve dips in large red or yellow bell peppers surrounded by vegetables for dipping.

2 cups mayonnaise

2 cups sour cream

3 tablespoons dill weed

3 tablespoons grated onion

1 tablespoon chopped parsley

1 teaspoon The Crown's Sassy Seasoning (page 218) or seasoned salt

Juice of 1 lemon

A loaf rye bread, Hawaiian bread, or any crusty bread

1) In a large bowl, combine mayonnaise and sour cream. Add dill, onion, parsley, Sassy Seasoning, and lemon juice; mix thoroughly. Refrigerate at least 24 hours before serving. Keeps well for 3–4 days.

2) Cut top part off bread. Using a sharp knife, hollow bread to make a bowl, saving the bread that you cut out.

3) To serve, spoon dip into bread bowl, and surround with pieces of reserved bread.

TIP: To make bell pepper bowls, lay peppers on flattest side. Leaving stem on (for looks), cut a slice from the top to create a "bowl." Remove membranes and seeds from inside bell pepper; wash and dry. Place in plastic bag until ready to fill with dip. Cut the top into long pieces to use for dipping. An eggplant also makes a colorful dipping "bowl."

HOT VIDALIA ONION DIP

MAKES 3 CUPS.

This hot dip is so good that sometimes I call it a vegetable and serve it for supper!

1 (8-ounce) package cream cheese, cubed, softened

3 tablespoons mayonnaise

5 ounces Parmesan cheese, freshly grated

3 Vidalia or sweet onions, chopped

1) In a bowl, thoroughly combine cream cheese, mayonnaise, and Parmesan. Mix in onions until blended.

2) Very lightly butter a baking dish; then add onion mixture. Bake in preheated 350° oven 45 minutes.

3) Serve hot with corn chips, tortilla chips, or toasted bread rounds. (May be made ahead, and refrigerated until ready to serve.)

TIDBIT: Sweet Vidalia onions from Georgia start arriving in markets in the spring, and they are a joy to use. They don't make your eyes water, don't give you onion breath, and they are scrumptious simply roasted in the oven with a little butter. If you can't find Vidalia or other sweet onions, I've made this recipe with ordinary yellow onions, and still love the flavor.

CHUNKY COLD ARTICHOKE DIP

MAKES 3 CUPS.

I am guilty of always making more of a dish than I need when I'm cooking for a group. It is against my religion to run out of anything at a cocktail buffet or in The Crown. So, when half the guests didn't show at a party, I was left with a lot of artichoke dip, and Artichoke Chicken (page 112) was created. It is now one of the revolving specials on the menu, and a great favorite served over rice with all the juices.

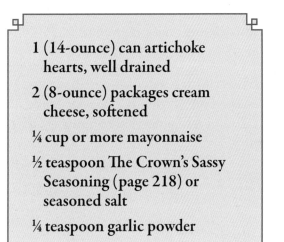

1 (14-ounce) can artichoke hearts, well drained

2 (8-ounce) packages cream cheese, softened

¼ cup or more mayonnaise

½ teaspoon The Crown's Sassy Seasoning (page 218) or seasoned salt

¼ teaspoon garlic powder

1) Cut artichokes into small pieces. Transfer to a plate to drain. Set aside.

2) Mix cream cheese and mayonnaise in electric mixing bowl.

3) Add artichokes, Sassy Seasoning, and garlic powder, and continue to mix. If you desire a softer texture for spreading on crackers, add a bit more mayonnaise. Taste, and adjust seasonings as desired.

4) Use immediately, or refrigerate 3–4 days. Serve on crackers, spooned into tiny filo cups, or spread on rounds of brown bread as an open-face sandwich, sprinkled with paprika.

Chunky Cold Artichoke Dip

BLUE CHEESE CARAWAY DIP

MAKES 2 CUPS.

In 1976, when we opened The Crown, we served this dip in a small bowl with crackers around it at every table. We think a little something savory perks the appetite, and you enjoy lunch more. We still sample appetizers in the gift shop with our Taste of Gourmet products. You never leave The Crown hungry, and some of our regular customers still ask for this dip!

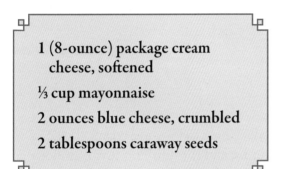

1 (8-ounce) package cream cheese, softened

⅓ cup mayonnaise

2 ounces blue cheese, crumbled

2 tablespoons caraway seeds

1) Combine cream cheese and mayonnaise in mixing bowl, and blend well.

2) Add blue cheese and caraway seeds, and continue mixing until well blended.

3) Dip can be served immediately, but flavors become stronger when refrigerated for several hours. Dip will keep well for 4–5 days, and can be doubled or tripled easily.

4) Serve with crackers, or fresh vegetables, such as carrot sticks, celery sticks, cucumber slices, or zucchini slices.

Janice's Hot Crawfish Dip

SERVES 8–10 AS AN APPETIZER.

If any is left after your guests have gone, plan to enjoy it the next day or so, served over rice or pasta as your main dish. Incredibly good and easy to make!

1 stick unsalted butter

1 bunch green onions, sliced

1 small green bell pepper, diced

1 small red bell pepper, diced

1 (1-pound) package frozen crawfish tails, thawed, undrained

2 cloves garlic, minced

1 tablespoon Creole seasoning (Tony's or Zatarain's)

1 (8-ounce) package cream cheese, softened

Dash of Tabasco

1) Melt butter in large saucepan over medium heat. Stir in onions and bell peppers, and continue cooking until bell peppers are just tender.

2) Add crawfish with juices, garlic, and Creole seasoning, and cook about 10 minutes, stirring occasionally.

3) Reduce heat to low, add cream cheese in chunks, and stir until mixture is smooth and bubbly. Taste, and if it isn't spicy enough, add more Tabasco; stir well.

4) Serve immediately, or cool, and refrigerate for 2–3 days. Warm slowly over low heat, stirring constantly. Serve with thin slices of toasted French bread baguettes or Melba toast for dipping.

TIDBIT: For the "Blues at Home" art exhibit at the B.B. King Museum, we wanted everything we served to be "Delta!" The menu was simple: Hot Crawfish Dip, Pickled Black-Eyed Peas, Hot Tamales (cut in half and arranged on a bed of the cooked husks—it looked like a huge sunflower), and Smokey Catfish Torta. All the recipes are in the book, so you can throw a "Mississippi Delta" party at your house!

SENSATIONAL SHRIMP DIP

MAKES 2 CUPS.

Perfect dip when you are in a hurry—smooth, piquant, and delicious. Serve with chips or crackers any time you are hungry for something cool!

1 cup sour cream

1 (8-ounce) package cream cheese, softened

½ cup finely diced celery

½ cup finely diced green onions

Juice of 1 lemon

½ teaspoon salt

½ teaspoon white pepper

Pinch of cayenne

Dash of Tabasco

2 (6-ounce) cans shrimp, drained

1) In a bowl, thoroughly combine sour cream and cream cheese.

2) Add celery, onions, lemon, salt, white pepper, cayenne, and Tabasco, and mix well.

3) Gently fold in shrimp. Cover, and refrigerate until needed.

DEVILED CHEESE BALL

SERVES 16–18.

Mississippi Blues legend, Robert Johnson, is said to have sold his soul to the Devil at the Crossroads to be a better guitar player. Blues music has always been called "the Devil's music" by good churchgoing people. But we still love Deviled Ham, Deviled Eggs, and the Blues in the dusty Mississippi Delta.

2 (8-ounce) packages cream cheese, softened

8 ounces sharp cheese, grated

1 (4¼-ounce) can Deviled Ham

2 teaspoons Worcestershire

2 teaspoons grated onion

1 teaspoon The Crown's Sassy Seasoning (page 218) or seasoned salt

2 tablespoons chopped pimento

2 tablespoons parsley flakes

1 tablespoon paprika

½–1 cup toasted pecans, whole or chopped

1) Combine cream cheese and Cheddar in mixing bowl.

2) Add ham, Worcestershire, onion, Sassy Seasoning, pimento, parsley, and paprika, and mix thoroughly.

3) Chill 1–2 hours. Form into a ball, then roll in pecans.

4) Cover tightly with plastic wrap, and refrigerate until ready to serve.

B.B.'s Pickled Black-Eyed Peas

SERVES 12–20.

Tart, sweet, and healthy, this should be made a week ahead of time so the flavors pickle perfectly. Love it with corn chips as an appetizer, but also wonderful as a salad or side dish with a meal. Makes a lot, but you won't waste a bite!

1½ cups sugar

2 teaspoons salt

1 teaspoon coarsely ground black pepper

1 cup oil

1¾ cups apple cider vinegar

½ teaspoon dry mustard

1 large onion, diced

1 large green bell pepper, diced

1 small red bell pepper, diced

2 (15-ounce) cans black-eyed peas

2 (15-ounce) cans crowder peas or field peas

2 (15-ounce) cans pinto beans

1) In a large bowl, combine sugar, salt, black pepper, oil, vinegar, and mustard, and stir well. Add onion and bell peppers, and mix marinade well.

2) Carefully rinse peas and beans under running water, and drain well. Add to marinade, and stir gently several times before covering and refrigerating. Flavor is best when it sits overnight and can be held refrigerated for a week before serving.

3) Serve with scoop-style corn chips.

TIDBIT: Gallons of pickled black-eyed peas were served with corn chips at the B.B. King Museum in August of 2014 for the opening reception of the "Blues at Home" art exhibit. H.C. Porter from Vicksburg, Mississippi, exhibited her original paintings of thirty Mississippi blues artists with an audio of each talking about their music and life. Many of the musicians were at the reception sitting in front of their own painting and talking to people. It was a once-in-a-lifetime event to have that many famous blues musicians in one place! Later that night, the musicians played together at historic Club Ebony, just around the corner from the museum.

Opening reception of the "Blues at Home" art exhibit.

B.B.'s Pickled Black-Eyed Peas

BITE-SIZE BACON QUICHE

MAKES 24.

Make these for cocktail parties, dinner parties, or bridal teas and showers. It's a great make-ahead fancy appetizer, and I promise there will be many compliments.

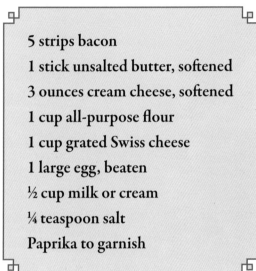

5 strips bacon

1 stick unsalted butter, softened

3 ounces cream cheese, softened

1 cup all-purpose flour

1 cup grated Swiss cheese

1 large egg, beaten

½ cup milk or cream

¼ teaspoon salt

Paprika to garnish

1) Fry bacon crisp, and drain.

2) In a bowl, cream butter and cream cheese. Add flour, and work it in with fingers. Roll dough into a ball, and chill (this can be done a day ahead).

3) When ready to bake, lightly spray or butter miniature muffin tins. Divide dough into 24 balls, and press each one into a muffin cup and up the side a bit, making tiny pastry shells.

4) Place cheese in each shell, dividing it evenly and using it all. Crumble bacon, and put on top, using it all. Mix egg, milk, and salt, then spoon mixture into each shell, using it all. Sprinkle each quiche with paprika.

5) Bake in preheated 350° oven 25–30 minutes. Serve warm. (Quiche can be baked and frozen for a week; just bring to room temperature, and warm quickly in hot oven.)

BROWN SUGAR BACON WITH CHOCOLATE

SERVES 8–10.

Bacon makes a great appetizer, passed at a party, or stacked like logs on a buffet—and who doesn't love bacon? Make without the chocolate for a more savory appetizer.

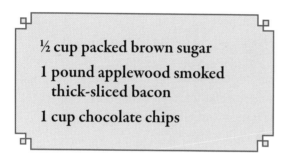

½ cup packed brown sugar

1 pound applewood smoked thick-sliced bacon

1 cup chocolate chips

TIDBIT: Tony and I have always enjoyed brunch at the Peabody Hotel in Memphis, Tennessee. When we went for our 50th anniversary, I loved the chocolate dipped bacon sprinkled with finely chopped pecans on their dessert buffet. When I tried it at home, I preferred the pure chocolate, but you might want to try it with the pecans.

1) Cover a baking sheet completely in aluminum foil, and place a large rack on top. Place brown sugar in large plastic bag. Add bacon strips to bag, a few at a time, and shake well to coat bacon. Place coated bacon on rack with a little space between each. Continue with remaining bacon. Raise oven rack to top level. Cook bacon in preheated 375° oven 18–20 minutes. Set aside to cool, then cut pieces in half.

2) Melt chocolate chips in small saucepan; remove from heat. Dip one end of bacon into chocolate. Place bacon on rack until chocolate is firm. Serve stacked on a serving plate as a pick-up dessert. Bacon holds well for several hours.

SPICY BEEF SKEWERS

SERVES 8–16.

I love these skewers warm on a bed of cold Tangy Cucumber and Onions (page 73) as a first course for dinner parties. It's an easily passed appetizer that works well piled into a shallow bowl, meat inside bowl, sticks pointed up, on a buffet table. We served this to B.B. King at the museum's ground breaking ceremony in 2006, along with lots of other great food. I loved serving B.B. as he sat in his cozy arm chair and enjoyed the festivities, along with a glass of water (with no ice).

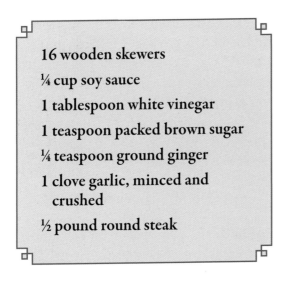

16 wooden skewers

¼ cup soy sauce

1 tablespoon white vinegar

1 teaspoon packed brown sugar

¼ teaspoon ground ginger

1 clove garlic, minced and crushed

½ pound round steak

1) Soak wooden skewers in water, and refrigerate at least 1 hour. This will help prevent wood from burning during cooking.

2) For marinade, combine soy sauce, vinegar, sugar, ginger, and garlic in a bowl. Stir well to dissolve sugar. Set aside.

3) Cut beef into finger-length strips about ¼ inch thick. Thread each strip lengthwise onto a skewer. Place on a cookie sheet with sides, and drizzle marinade over skewers. Turn to season each side of meat. Cover, and refrigerate several hours or overnight.

4) When ready to serve, place cookie sheet under a hot broiler 3 minutes on each side, turning once. Serve warm or cold.

Tony and Evelyn with B.B. King

Spicy Beef Skewers

PORK BITES IN SESAME SEEDS

MAKES 20–25 BITES.

These deliciously exotic bites are a wonderful appetizer with the crunch of sesame seeds against the hot or sweet mustard. Easy to pass around, and fun for guests to dip each bite.

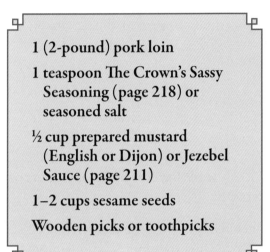

1 (2-pound) pork loin

1 teaspoon The Crown's Sassy Seasoning (page 218) or seasoned salt

½ cup prepared mustard (English or Dijon) or Jezebel Sauce (page 211)

1–2 cups sesame seeds

Wooden picks or toothpicks

1) Place pork loin in baking dish, rub with Sassy Seasoning, and bake at 350° for 1 hour or until done. (Pork can be cooked several days before serving, wrapped, and refrigerated.)

2) Toast sesame seeds by placing in a large stainless skillet on medium heat, stirring constantly to brown evenly—careful not to burn. (Seeds will keep tightly sealed for weeks.)

3) Place mustard and toasted sesame seeds in 2 separate bowls. Slice pork roast into finger-size pieces. Insert wooden pick, dip about ½ inch into mustard, then dip into sesame seeds. Place on serving platter, making a circle on the outer edge of the platter, with meat toward center. Make second circle inside first ones with pick sticking up and propped on first circle.

TIDBIT: A cocktail party at a friend's house in Thailand introduced us to this great appetizer. When we lived in England, we used English mustard, but that was too intense for friends when we came home. So now we usually use Jezebel Sauce (page 211)—that sweet hot, horseradish mustard made with fruit that is a staple in southern homes during the holidays—I keep it in my refrigerator year-round.

VARIATIONS: Let guests dip their own. Substitute cooked ham for the pork.

MAMA'S CHICKEN DRUMETTES

SERVES 8 AS AN APPETIZER.

Before "wings were the thing," Mama was cooking these drumettes for our parties. Messy delicious fun for everyone, and not spicy!

¼ **cup prepared mustard**

1 tablespoon butter, melted

1 tablespoon honey

1 tablespoon Worcestershire

1 tablespoon grated onion

1 teaspoon salt

¼ **teaspoon finely ground black pepper**

24 chicken drumettes

1) In a bowl, place mustard, butter, honey, Worcestershire, onion, salt, and black pepper. Mix thoroughly, and set aside.

2) Wash drumettes, and dry thoroughly. Rub mixture on each drumette, covering it completely. Arrange in large baking pan. Seasoned chicken can be covered and kept in the refrigerator for several hours or overnight.

3) When ready to serve, bake in preheated 350° oven 30–40 minutes until lightly browned.

TIDBIT: We grew up cutting up whole chickens and using every bit of it in some way. Mama's recipe even explained in detail how to cut the skin at the joint, leaving as much skin on drumette as possible, and also suggested saving the wingtip portion for making stock. We would both save drumettes in the freezer until we had enough to cook a batch. Later we could buy the drumettes, and we made these more often.

SHRIMP RÉMOULADE

SERVES 8–10.

Spicy and delicious, Shrimp Rémoulade is enjoyed across the South at parties mounded on a lettuce-lined platter, and in restaurants piled on shredded lettuce garnished with tomato, boiled egg quarters, and a wedge of lemon. You know it's a party when rémoulade is served!

3 cloves garlic, peeled

¼ teaspoon salt

1 cup mayonnaise

⅓ cup Creole mustard or Dijon

⅓ cup horseradish

1 tablespoon lemon juice

½ cup ketchup

1 tablespoon Worcestershire

3 green onions, finely chopped

3 drops Tabasco (or to taste)

2 pounds medium shrimp, raw

2 teaspoons crab boil

2 bay leaves

1) Mince garlic cloves, sprinkle with salt, and smash with side of knife until garlic is almost "melted."

2) Combine garlic, mayonnaise, mustard, horseradish, lemon juice, ketchup, and Worcestershire. Stir in onions and Tabasco. Sauce can be made a day ahead, tightly covered and refrigerated.

3) Place shrimp in large cooking pot, and cover with water; add crab boil and bay leaves, and heat on high just until water comes to a boil. Immediately take pot off heat, and allow shrimp to cool in seasoned water.

4) Remove cooled shrimp from water, peel, and devein. Place shrimp in large bowl; pour sauce over shrimp, stirring gently to combine. Cover tightly, and refrigerate for up to 3 days.

5) Serve well chilled.

TIDBIT: This traditional Louisiana dish has its origins in France like so many New Orleans specialties. My uncle made gallons of Shrimp Rémoulade for his daughter's wedding reception—not a shrimp was left.

PICKLED SHRIMP REGINA

SERVES 20–24 AS AN APPETIZER.

So good and flavorful, you may never eat plain boiled shrimp again. It gets better after several days of pickling. Perfect for a large party, because it can be made ahead, and it is beautiful!

1 (3-ounce) box Zatarain's or other crab boil

5 pounds shrimp, medium to large, peeled and deveined

1⅓ cups oil

1 cup white vinegar

1 cup prepared salsa

2 tablespoons mustard

2 tablespoons Tabasco

1 tablespoon paprika

2 tablespoons Worcestershire

3 tablespoons capers

2 tablespoons garlic powder

1 teaspoon celery seeds

1 teaspoon salt

1 teaspoon coarsely ground black pepper

1) Put crab boil into a large pot of water, and bring to a hard boil. Add shrimp, let water come back to a boil, and cook 3 minutes. Do not overcook! Take pan off heat, and let shrimp cool in seasoned water. Peel shrimp.

2) In a large bowl, thoroughly combine oil, vinegar, salsa, mustard, Tabasco, paprika, Worcestershire, capers, garlic powder, celery seeds, salt, and black pepper. This marinade will flavor up to 5 pounds of shrimp; if you cook less shrimp, do not cut down on marinade. You can triple (or more) the recipe for a big crowd.

3) Cover cooked, peeled shrimp with marinade, and refrigerate at least 24 hours. Stir or turn shrimp in marinade daily for best flavor. Pickled Shrimp will keep for a week refrigerated—and they just get better.

4) To serve, lift shrimp out of marinade, and pile into a large bowl on buffet table.

TIDBIT: We created this deliciously flavorful dish for our niece Regina's wedding and served it at many weddings and parties in the Delta.

CAPERED CATFISH BITES

SERVES 20–24 AS AN APPETIZER.

Serve these sharply flavorful bites scattered on a bed of lettuce as a salad, or insert wooden picks and pass around on a tray. The fish is firm, and the caper dressing—delicious!

1 cup olive oil

¾ cup white vinegar

¼ cup sugar

2½ teaspoons salt, divided

1 teaspoon dry mustard

5 bay leaves, divided

2 cloves garlic, minced

2 teaspoons chopped parsley

¼ cup capers, drained

3 cups water

½ white onion, thinly sliced

Juice of 1 fresh lemon

½ teaspoon black pepper

8 U.S. Farm-Raised Catfish
   fillets, cut into 1-inch pieces

1) In a large glass bowl, combine oil, vinegar, sugar, 2 teaspoons salt, mustard, 3 bay leaves, garlic, parsley, and capers, and mix well. Set this marinade aside.

2) Put water in large saucepan; add onion, lemon juice, black pepper, remaining ½ teaspoon salt, and remaining 2 bay leaves. Bring to a simmer, and add catfish pieces, poaching gently in seasoned water. Do not crowd fish, and keep water at a simmer. Cook about 5 minutes. Using slotted spoon, remove fish from water, and set aside to drain.

3) Carefully put cooked catfish into marinade; gently stir to cover all pieces. Cover, and refrigerate at least 4 hours, or overnight. Keeps well 4–5 days.

4) When ready to serve, drain marinade. Serve at a cocktail buffet in a shallow bowl as a pick-up appetizer, speared with wooden picks.

VARIATION: Substitute peeled shrimp for the catfish.

TIDBIT: At a party honoring B.B. King before the museum opened, we served this in tiny toast cups to rave reviews. Cut slices of brown bread into 4 pieces, brush with melted butter, press into mini muffin tins, and bake at 350° until toasted. Place toast cups on a tray, and top with a Capered Catfish Bites.

SMOKY CATFISH TORTA

SERVES 25 ON COCKTAIL BUFFET.

We've served this torta at a governor's inauguration party, local parties, wedding receptions, and at the B.B. King Museum for a number of events. The blend of flavors is wonderful, the smoke is subtle, and the texture is varied. Serve it with water crackers or toasted pita triangles (piled on a tray beneath the cake plate), and scoop up every bite!

2 (8-ounce) packages cream cheese, softened

Juice of 2 lemons

2 teaspoons Tabasco

2 cups diced catfish or other fish, smoked or grilled

4 green onions, finely chopped

2–3 tablespoons capers, drained

1 hard-boiled egg, minced (optional)

Lemon slices and mint or parsley to garnish

1) Beat cream cheese, lemon juice, and Tabasco with electric mixer until light and fluffy.

2) On a footed cake stand or serving plate, place ⅓ of cream cheese mixture. Smooth and flatten, keeping it at least 2 inches inside rim of serving plate. Sprinkle ⅓ of diced catfish evenly on top of cream cheese mixture. Add ⅓ of green onions and a sprinkling of capers.

3) Add another layer of ⅓ of cream cheese mixture on top, then layer with catfish, onions, and capers.

4) Repeat for third layer.

5) Cover tightly, and refrigerate for several hours or overnight, if possible.

6) When ready to serve, sprinkle top of torta with eggs, if desired, and a bit more capers. Garnish edge of cake stand with lemon slices and mint or parsley.

CRAWFISH BEIGNETS

MAKES ABOUT 50.

A cream puff pastry with crawfish and spices. In the South, we do love our fried foods, and this is beyond delicious! You may vary it by using finely chopped shrimp or fish fillets instead of crawfish—equally delicious!

1 cup water

6 tablespoons unsalted butter, in pieces

1 teaspoon cayenne pepper

Pinch of nutmeg

1 cup all-purpose flour

4 eggs

¾ pound crawfish, thawed and drained

2 tablespoons chopped chives

2 drops Tabasco

1 tablespoon Italian seasoning

Oil for frying

Parmesan cheese to garnish

1) Bring water, butter, cayenne pepper, and nutmeg to a boil in a large, heavy saucepan. Boil slowly until butter melts. Remove from heat, and immediately add flour, stirring vigorously until well blended.

2) Put pan back on heat, and cook a few minutes, beating continuously, until mixture is smooth and pulls away from side of pan. Remove from heat, and beat in eggs, one at a time, fully incorporating into mixture before adding next egg. Set pastry mixture aside.

3) Chop crawfish finely to make 1 cup. Pat with paper towels to remove excess moisture. Add to pastry mixture with chives, Tabasco, and Italian seasoning, and mix thoroughly.

4) Heat oil to a good frying temperature (365°). Drop beignets into hot oil using a rounded ½ teaspoon as a measure. They will be fairly small and will cook quickly. Cook until lightly browned; sprinkle with Parmesan cheese. Serve immediately.

5) Beignets are still good when served cold; but like any fried food, hot is best.

SESAME CHEESE STRAWS

MAKES 50–60.

The sesame seeds are my delicious addition to this basic cheese straw recipe.

1 (8-ounce) block sharp Cheddar cheese

1 stick unsalted butter, softened

½ teaspoon cayenne pepper

1 level teaspoon sugar

½ teaspoon salt

1¼ cups all-purpose flour

½ cup sesame seeds (optional)

1) Grate cheese, using small holes on grater. In large mixing bowl, thoroughly combine cheese and butter. Add cayenne pepper, sugar, and salt; mix well.

2) Stir in flour in 2 batches, mixing well after each addition. Add sesame seeds, if you choose, and mix thoroughly.

3) Use a cookie press or cake decorator to pipe mixture onto cookie sheets in long strips. Score strips into finger-length pieces so they will separate nicely after they are baked.

4) Bake in preheated 350° oven 8–10 minutes until set, but not browned. Watch carefully. (I tend to overcook the first batch, but enjoy eating them anyway.)

TIDBIT: This recipe was given to the Delta by Mrs. Josephine Connor of Indianola in 1982, when she published *I Promised a Cookbook*, a lifetime collection of her recipes. She was the caterer for all occasions until she retired at age 87. Mrs. Connor always autographed her books that we sold at The Crown, and was still calling to see if we needed more when she was 101. She was a true Delta lady who loved cooking, people, and parties.

JEN'S BOURBON LIME SLUSH

MAKES ABOUT 5 CUPS.

We love for my daughter Jen to make this icy drink, especially in the summer, when we can sit on the deck and cool off. Cypress trees and knees are everywhere on the lake bank, blue herons and ducks put on a show for us, and the sunset on the lake is so peaceful. . . .

1 (6-ounce) can frozen limeade, thawed

6 ounces bourbon

Fresh mint, a nice handful

Ice

Sprigs of mint to garnish

1) Pour limeade and bourbon into blender.

2) Wash mint, pick leaves off stems, then add mint leaves to blender. Blend to mix completely.

3) With blender on, carefully add ice cubes one at a time, until blender is ¾ full.

4) Serve immediately in Julep cups or wine glasses with a spring of mint to garnish.

MOCK MINT JULEP

MAKES 6.

Delicious punch to serve at a party, for kids and adults. I always freeze some extra syrup mixture a day ahead in molds (with slices of lemon and mint leaves) to float in the punch bowl. Pretty decoration, keeps punch cold, and doesn't dilute the flavor.

¾ cup frozen lemon juice

¾ cup white Karo syrup

1 (32-ounce) bottle ginger ale (or Sprite)

Fresh mint leaves

Lemon slices

1) Vigorously mix lemon juice and Karo syrup in a pitcher. Set aside for 2–3 hours.

2) When ready to serve, add ginger ale, and stir lightly. (Do not add ginger ale earlier because it will lose the fizz!)

3) Garnish each glass or Julep cup with fresh mint and a lemon slice on the edge, or pour into punch bowl to serve.

DELTA MILK PUNCH

SERVES 20–25.

This has been a Christmas Eve tradition in our family for as long as I can remember. When I was little, I wondered why the kids weren't given glasses of milk like the grown-ups had—now I know. My sister Wanda makes it full strength, but I usually cut the amount of bourbon in half, and it tastes wonderful, and gets even better after a day in the refrigerator. Egg nog is good, but smooth Delta Milk Punch is wonderful.

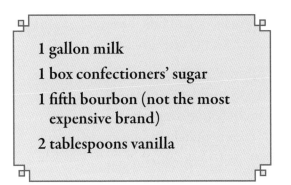

1 gallon milk

1 box confectioners' sugar

1 fifth bourbon (not the most expensive brand)

2 tablespoons vanilla

1) Pour milk into a large 2-gallon container, and sprinkle confectioners' sugar over milk. Stir vigorously until sugar is completely dissolved.

2) Add bourbon and vanilla, and continue stirring until well mixed. (Taste, and add more vanilla, if you choose.)

3) Cover, and refrigerate until very cold before serving. Milk punch keeps well in the refrigerator for several days.

4) Serve from glass pitchers or a punch bowl.

Summer Tea

MAKES 1 GALLON.

We call it Summer Tea, but in the Mississippi Delta, we drink it at all kinds of parties all during the year, and it's often served at wedding receptions. It's a bit more festive than plain sweet tea, so it isn't usually part of a family dinner…though the children love the citrus flavor.

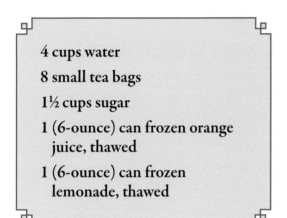

4 cups water

8 small tea bags

1½ cups sugar

1 (6-ounce) can frozen orange juice, thawed

1 (6-ounce) can frozen lemonade, thawed

1) Bring water to a boil in large saucepan. Add tea bags, and boil 1 minute. Turn off heat, and let tea steep.

2) While tea is still warm, remove tea bags, and add sugar, stirring to dissolve. Add juices to tea, stirring well.

3) Pour tea into a 1-gallon pitcher, and add enough water to make a gallon.

4) Refrigerate until ready to serve. Serve over ice.

TIDBIT: I also call it Garden Club Tea, because I was given the recipe to serve at a garden club luncheon in 1976. Town and Country Garden Club was Mama's club, and after she died, the club asked me to join. I was touched, and I'm still a member, and serve the tea regularly for events. When the "Born on the Bayou" Harmony Guitar was unveiled in the park next door to The Crown, we served Summer Tea to everyone who came while the guitar player entertained on a lovely spring evening.

BREAD & BRUNCH

Caramel Baked French Toast

Mama's Buttermilk Cornbread

SERVES 4–6.

Nothing is better with a bowl of soup than a pan of hot cornbread. Whether you crumble it into the bowl, or butter it and eat it on the side. You'll notice that our family doesn't put sugar in our cornbread. I can eat it "sweetened," but in the Delta, we like it plain— and we eat our cake for dessert!

1½ cups white self-rising cornmeal

½ cup self-rising flour

½ teaspoon baking powder

1 egg

1 cup buttermilk

2 tablespoons vegetable oil

1) Preheat oven to 425°. In a bowl, combine cornmeal, flour, baking powder, egg, and buttermilk, stirring vigorously to blend.

2) Heat oil in 9-inch oven-proof skillet on medium heat, and roll around skillet to coat bottom and side. Pour cornbread mixture into hot skillet, and immediately place in hot oven.

3) Bake cornbread about 20 minutes, or until nicely browned. Invert onto a plate, cut, and enjoy every bite!

TIDBIT: One of my daddy's favorite snacks after supper was a glass of cold milk with cold cornbread crumbled into it! I love it, too. I usually wrap up the leftover bread and enjoy it the next afternoon while I'm cooking supper! It's just a little southern appetizer.

TIP: If you don't have buttermilk, stir 1 teaspoon white vinegar into 1 cup of milk, let it sit for 5 minutes, then add to mixture.

40

MAMA'S HUSHPUPPIES

MAKES ABOUT 20.

Hushpuppies are the traditional "bread" to serve with fried fish. And in the Delta, that means catfish! A fish fry is happening somewhere in the Delta all the time to raise money for churches, clubs, or for people in need. The menu is always the same: Fried catfish, hushpuppies, French fries, and coleslaw. That's a perfect Delta fish fry.

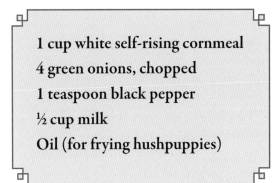

1 cup white self-rising cornmeal

4 green onions, chopped

1 teaspoon black pepper

½ cup milk

Oil (for frying hushpuppies)

TIDBIT: Try the hushpuppies as a snack for a football party; just keep them warm in a tightly closed brown paper sack. That brown paper sack is another southern secret. It keeps fried food warm, and drains the "grease" at the same time. Mama didn't wait until she was frying fish to make hushpuppies. She made them anytime she was hungry for them. We had them with vegetables instead of cornbread, with BBQ and ham, and just as a snack sometimes. Hushpuppies are good eating!

1) In a small bowl, mix cornmeal, onions, and black pepper. Add milk, and mix thoroughly. Let sit for a few minutes while the oil is heating, but don't stir the batter.

2) Heat 1-inch of oil in skillet or pan, and make sure it is hot before starting to drop hushpuppies.

3) Using a teaspoon, scoop out a rounded spoonful of hushpuppy batter. Lightly roll and mash it against side of bowl on one side and then the other. (This will compress the mixture slightly and prevent the hushpuppy from falling apart in the hot oil.) Using another teaspoon, push the hushpuppy off the spoon into the hot oil. Work quickly to fry 6 or 8 at a time, but do not crowd them.

4) Fry until browned, remove with slotted spoon, drain, and serve hot!

FRUIT TEA BREAD

SERVES 6–8.

When we moved to the English village of Pakenham, Suffolk, Betty Birkby was one of the first people to come by to welcome us! She brought us a jar of her homemade marmalade and an invitation to tea the next afternoon. Our families became great friends, taking excursions together, and eating together often. This is one of Betty's specialties, and I've served it many times at an English Afternoon Tea at The Crown. I love it for breakfast with a little smear of butter.

1 cup milk

1 cup All-Bran cereal

1 cup dried fruit (raisins, cranberries, currants)

1 cup packed brown sugar

1 cup self-rising flour

1) Combine milk and All-Bran in a small bowl. Set aside to soak 2–12 hours.

2) Combine fruit, sugar, and flour. Stir milk mixture into flour mixture, and mix thoroughly. The batter will be stiff. Pour batter into sprayed large loaf pan. Bake in preheated 300° oven until center is set, about 75 minutes.

3) Tea bread is very moist and quite dense, almost like a fruit cake. I like to cut a slice, and then cut that slice into 2 or 3 bite-size pieces to serve on a plate, plain or with a dab of butter or cream cheese on top. It will keep for 2 weeks on the counter, if you can stay out of this healthy, delicious bread.

The Crown's Crêpes

MAKES 20–24.

Crêpes are one of the most requested dishes for special parties at The Crown, sometimes as sweet Delicious Dessert Crêpes topped with fruit (page 197) or as a savory main dish, Chicken and Mushroom Crêpes (page 127). These light French pancakes also make a simple breakfast or snack, sprinkled with a bit of powdered sugar or spread with jam.

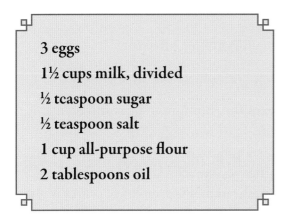

3 eggs

1½ cups milk, divided

½ tcaspoon sugar

½ teaspoon salt

1 cup all-purpose flour

2 tablespoons oil

TIP: The first crêpe you cook in a batch is just to test the heat and amount you need to put in the pan.

1) With electric mixer, beat eggs with 1 cup milk, sugar, and salt. Gradually add flour, beating well. Slowly add remaining ½ cup milk and oil, and beat several minutes until smooth. If possible, allow to rest before using. (Can be refrigerated 2 days, tightly covered, with plastic wrap on top of batter.)

2) When ready to cook, lightly coat 8-inch crêpe pan or nonstick skillet with oil. Heat skillet to medium, then pour about 2 tablespoons batter into skillet, quickly turning and rolling skillet to completely cover bottom, not side. Crêpe should be very thin and will cook very quickly. (If a hole appears, "patch" it with a drop of batter.) When edges are cooked, carefully flip crêpe over for just a few seconds. The crêpe should stay pliable and soft.

3) Remove crêpe from pan, and place on a kitchen towel while continuing to cook remaining crêpes, stacking them on top of each other in 2 or 3 stacks. Cover with towel, wrap in plastic wrap, and refrigerate until needed, up to 4 days. Or freeze for up to a week, if very tightly wrapped.

ORANGE BREAKFAST RING

SERVES 6–8.

Delicious for breakfast or brunch and wonderful when friends come by for coffee in the morning! This great pull-apart bread can be sliced, and tastes more like cake than biscuits. If some is left, cut slices, butter lightly, and toast under broiler. My grandson Prescott has fun dipping the biscuits for me. (Boys do love things that are messy.)

1 cup sugar

3 tablespoons grated orange rind

⅓ cup butter

2 (12-ounce) cans buttermilk biscuits

1 (3-ounce) package cream cheese, softened

½ cup powdered sugar

2 tablespoons orange juice

1) Preheat oven to 350°. Lightly butter a 9-inch Bundt or tube pan.

2) Melt butter in a bowl in microwave.

3) In another bowl, mix sugar and orange rind.

4) Dip each biscuit in melted butter, then in sugar mixture.

5) Stand each biscuit on its side in tube pan, making a circle. Bake about 30 minutes, until nicely browned. When ring is baked, turn onto a serving plate.

6) While ring is baking, thoroughly combine cream cheese, powdered sugar, and orange juice. Spread over ring, and serve immediately.

VARIATION: For a smaller ring, use just 1 can of biscuits, but keep other ingredients the same.

Orange Breakfast Ring

Caramel Baked French Toast

SERVES 10.

1½ cups firmly packed brown sugar

2 sticks unsalted butter, divided

¼ cup plus 2 tablespoons light corn syrup

10–12 (1¾-inch-thick) slices French bread

4 eggs, beaten

1½ cups milk

1 cup whipping cream

¼ teaspoon salt

1 tablespoon vanilla

3 tablespoons sugar

1½ teaspoons cinnamon

1) In a small saucepan, place brown sugar, 1½ sticks butter, and corn syrup. Cook on medium heat, stirring constantly 5 minutes. Pour syrup mixture into lightly buttered 9x13-inch baking dish. Place bread slices over syrup to fill pan.

2) In a bowl, combine eggs, milk, cream, salt, and vanilla, stirring well. Slowly pour mixture over each bread slice. Cover, and chill at least 8 hours, or overnight.

3) In bowl, thoroughly combine sugar and cinnamon, then sprinkle evenly over soaked bread.

4) Melt remaining ¼ cup butter, and drizzle over bread.

5) Bake uncovered in preheated 350° oven 45–50 minutes, until browned and bubbly.

TIDBIT: This French toast was served to my sister-in-law Kay Roughton at a bed and breakfast many years ago, and the hostess graciously shared the recipe with her. We enjoyed it many times when we were with Bob and Kay, and Kay shared it with me. My copy is hiding in one of my four binders, filled with notes and recipes and menus. Thank goodness, Kay is better organized, and I have it in my kitchen again, and we are sharing it with you.

OPEN-FACED CRAB SANDWICHES

SERVES 6.

Mama and I loved serving these at parties. We could spread the crab mixture on muffin halves days ahead, and freeze them. On the day of the party, we thawed them on cookie sheets, refrigerated, until ready to broil. Serve as a luncheon or supper dish with a big salad.

1 stick unsalted butter, softened

1½ tablespoons mayonnaise

½ teaspoon garlic salt

½ teaspoon The Crown's Sassy Seasoning (page 218) or seasoned salt

1 (8-ounce) jar sharp Cheez Whiz or other processed cheese sauce

1 (6½-ounce) can crabmeat, drained

6 English muffins, split into halves

1) In a bowl, mix butter, mayonnaise, garlic salt, Sassy Seasoning, Cheez Whiz, and crabmeat. Stir together carefully.

2) Spread mixture equally on each muffin half. Put under broiler until bubbly hot. Serve warm.

VARIATION: To serve as an appetizer, cut each hot muffin half into six pie-shaped pieces before broiling. So easy, so tasty, and you can't eat just one!

The Crown's Fried Catfish Po'Boy with Comeback Sauce

SERVES 6–8.

BREAD

6–8 U.S. Farm-Raised Catfish fillets

1½ cups all-purpose flour

1½ teaspoons The Crown's Sassy Seasoning (page 218) or seasoned salt

Oil for frying

Po'Boy buns or hoagie buns

1 tablespoon butter

Comeback Sauce (page 210)

1) Wash catfish fillets, and set aside.

2) Mix flour and Sassy Seasoning in a shallow bowl. Place one fillet at a time in seasoned flour to dredge. and coat well on both sides. Set each aside on a cookie sheet as you coat the next one. (After all are coated, I always coat a second time.)

3) When all fillets are coated, heat 1 inch of oil in a large skillet. When oil is very hot (375°), place 3 or 4 fillets gently into oil, but do not crowd fish. Fry until fish are lightly browned, turning once. Drain first batch on paper towels, cover, and keep warm while cooking second batch of fish.

4) Lightly toast buns with a smidge of butter on each.

5) Just before serving, place fish fillets under a hot broiler for about 1 minute, then put fish on the bun spread with Comeback Sauce. Serve with shredded lettuce, tomato slices, and pickles for a delicious main dish sandwich, straight out of the Mississippi Delta.

SHRIMP SPRING ROLLS

MAKES 20 OR MORE.

We love serving these as appetizers, cooked just before guests arrive, and kept warm.

1 pound medium shrimp, cooked and peeled, without tail

½ cup ground pork, cooked

1 tablespoon finely chopped celery

1 tablespoon finely sliced green onion

½ teaspoon soy sauce

1 teaspoon sherry

1 teaspoon salt

¼ teaspoon finely ground black pepper

20–30 rice paper doilies (Asian grocery stores)

Oil for frying

1) Coarsely chop shrimp; place in bowl. Add pork, celery, onion, soy sauce, sherry, salt, and black pepper, and mix well. Refrigerate filling for several hours to blend flavors.

2) Place a rice paper doily on working surface. Place 2 tablespoons filling in middle of circle, making a log shape 3–4 inches long. Rub lightly with water to soften rice paper, then pull one side of circle to middle, touching one end of filling. Pull other side to middle, touching other end of filling. Rub a little water on the overlapping edges to seal. Pick up one end of the now rectangular doily, bring it up to the filling, sealing edges with water around filling. Then roll to end of the rice paper and seal with water. Set aside.

3) Continue rolling until all filling is used. Spring rolls can be refrigerated for several hours before frying.

4) When ready to serve, heat oil to 1-inch depth in heavy large skillet. When oil is hot, place 2 or 3 spring rolls in skillet and fry until rice paper is crisp, and lightly browned. Serve warm with Plum Sauce (page 212) or soy sauce mixed with green onions.

TIP: Rice paper doilies come in different sizes; the smaller ones are nicest for these spring rolls, but any size will work. We've enjoyed making these Shrimp Spring Rolls since living in Thailand, where we saw the doilies drying on bamboo screens propped against houses.

OVEN OMELET

SERVES 2.

Delicious as a special breakfast with fresh fruit or a quick light supper with a green salad. Everything can be prepared while the oven is heating, and is great for busy days or when you get home late and hungry!

3 eggs, separated

3 tablespoons cream

½ teaspoon The Crown's Sassy Seasoning (page 218) or seasoned salt

¾ teaspoon Italian seasoning

¼ teaspoon cream of tartar

¾ cup grated cheese (Cheddar, Swiss, etc.), divided

1 tablespoon butter

1) Preheat oven to 350°. Separate eggs, placing whites in electric mixing bowl and yolks in small bowl. To yolks, add cream, Sassy Seasoning, and Italian seasoning, and whisk well.

2) Beat egg whites with cream of tartar until stiff peaks form; fold in egg yolk mixture with half the grated cheese.

3) Melt butter in 9-inch oven-proof skillet on low heat, moving around to coat bottom and sides—do not let butter brown. Immediately add egg mixture, and cook on stove 2 minutes to set bottom. Transfer to hot oven; bake about 10 minutes.

4) Remove from oven, and sprinkle with remaining cheese. Cut in half, place on plates with spatula, and serve at once.

TIDBIT: I've used this recipe for 51 years, but the very first time, it was ill timed. We were newlyweds. I was excited about this recipe. Tony was coming in from the night shift at the base, and I had cooked a beautiful breakfast for him. He walked in the door and went straight to sleep. He didn't even taste it! I enjoyed it thoroughly, but I found out the hard way that "you eat when you wake up after the night shift, not before." He asks for the omelet for supper now, and eats every bite.

SAUSAGE BREAKFAST SOUFFLÉ

SERVES 8–10

This is a perfect dish for Thanksgiving or holiday breakfasts. Serve with fresh fruit, muffins, and maybe some cheese grits. It's a feast for breakfast that is often served at southern bed and breakfast homes and lovely hotels.

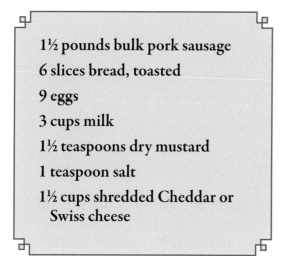

1½ pounds bulk pork sausage

6 slices bread, toasted

9 eggs

3 cups milk

1½ teaspoons dry mustard

1 teaspoon salt

1½ cups shredded Cheddar or Swiss cheese

1) Brown sausage on medium heat, stirring to crumble. Drain well, and set aside.

2) Cut each slice of toasted bread into 4 pieces, and set aside.

3) Place eggs in a large bowl, and beat well with a fork. Add sausage, milk, mustard, salt, and cheese, mixing well.

4) In a well-buttered 9x13-inch baking dish, place half the toast pieces on bottom of dish. Top with half the egg mixture. Layer with remaining toast and remaining egg mixture. Cover, and refrigerate for several hours, or overnight.

5) Bake in preheated 350° oven 1 hour. Serve warm.

THE CROWN'S
HAM AND SWISS QUICHE

SERVES 6–8.

Try using this recipe with cooked bacon for a classic Quiche Lorraine, or switch the cheese to Cheddar, Pepper Jack, Brie, or Camembert. Add cooked, diced shrimp or crabmeat. Be creative, and enjoy the results.

1 prepared pie crust

5 eggs, divided

1¼ cups heavy cream

1 cup grated Swiss cheese

3 ounces ham, finely chopped

1 tablespoon finely chopped green onion

½ teaspoon salt

Pinch of black pepper

Pinch of nutmeg

1 tablespoon unsalted butter

1) Prick crust with a fork on bottom and side. Bake in preheated 400° oven 10 minutes. Set aside.

2) Into a bowl, whisk 2 whole eggs and 3 egg yolks. (Save egg whites to make a Pavlova.) Stir in cream, and mix well.

3) Add cheese, ham, onion, salt, black pepper, and nutmeg, and mix well. Pour into pie crust, spreading cheese and ham evenly.

4) Dot with tiny pieces of butter.

5) Bake on lower rack in hot oven 35–40 minutes, or until puffed and lightly browned. Serve warm from the oven, if possible.

TIP: Quiche can be prepared and baked the day before serving, and refrigerated. Warm gently in a preheated 350° oven about 15 minutes to refresh.

SOUPS, STEWS & CHILIS

The Crown's Chicken and Sausage Gumbo

Farmer's Market Gazpacho

SERVES 8.

Enjoying fresh local vegetables in a flavorful cold soup on a hot summer day is Tony's idea of the perfect meal. Healthy and delicious!

SOUPS

1 cup peeled chopped tomatoes, or 1 (12-ounce) can petite diced tomatoes

1 green bell pepper, chopped

2 ribs celery, chopped

1 small cucumber, chopped

1 small onion, chopped

1 clove garlic, minced

3 cups tomato juice, divided

2 teaspoons chopped parsley

1 teaspoon chopped chives

3 tablespoons white vinegar

2 tablespoons olive oil

1 teaspoon salt

½ teaspoon coarsely ground black pepper

1 teaspoon Worcestershire

1) Place tomatoes, bell pepper, celery, cucumber, onion, and garlic in a bowl.

2) In a blender, put 1 cup of tomato juice and a third of the chopped vegetables. Turn on blender for a few spins to chop, but not pulverize, vegetables. Pour into a large bowl, and continue with remaining tomato juice and vegetables.

3) To vegetables, add parsley, chives, vinegar, olive oil, salt, black pepper, and Worcestershire. Stir well.

4) Refrigerate several hours before serving. Gazpacho will hold well 4–5 days.

TIDBIT: In the summer, when fresh vegetables are plentiful, we keep some gazpacho in the refrigerator. Tony fell in love with it in Spain while we were having lunch on a terrace at the Alhambra. On the first hot day of summer, Tony always asks for gazpacho!

Deanna's Meatball Soup

SERVES 6.

This soup combines wonderful flavors that make for a satisfying meal. It was shared with me by my daughter-in-law Deanna. Her children Izabela and Carter always ask if there will be "good bread" (crusty baguette) to go with it. Yes, indeed!

STOCK:

2 teaspoons olive oil

1 onion, chopped

3 carrots, peeled and chopped

3 celery stalks, chopped

½ teaspoon salt

¼ teaspoon ground black pepper

2 bay leaves

6 cups chicken broth

MEATBALLS:

1 (20-ounce) package ground turkey (or ground beef)

1 egg, beaten

2 cloves garlic, grated

½ teaspoon grated nutmeg

½ cup grated Parmigiano-Reggiano cheese

½ cup bread crumbs

SOUP FINISH:

1½ cups small pasta

5 ounces fresh baby spinach, cut

1 (15-ounce) can Great Northern beans, drained and rinsed

1) For Stock, heat olive oil in Dutch oven on medium. Add onion, carrots, celery, salt, black pepper, and bay leaves, and cook until vegetables soften, about 7 minutes. Add broth, increase heat to high, and bring to a boil.

2) For Meatballs, mix together by hand the meat, egg, garlic, nutmeg, cheese, and bread crumbs in a large bowl until just combined. Roll Meatballs about ¾ inch in diameter (kids love doing this part), and carefully drop them 1 at a time into boiling soup.

3) When all Meatballs have floated to top of pot, return soup to a boil, and stir in pasta. Reduce heat, cover, and simmer 10 minutes.

4) Remove bay leaves. Stir in spinach and beans, and cook 5 minutes. Taste, and adjust seasonings as desired. Serve hot.

TIDBIT: Our Meatball Soup is a variation on one served at Deanna's family weddings when she was growing up. Deanna uses any small pasta in the pantry instead of the traditional ditalini, and replaces the escarole with spinach. It's my grandchildren's favorite meal.

SOUPS

FRENCH ONION SOUP

SERVES 6.

This classic soup is served across the world, from France to New Orleans to Thailand, and Tony always orders it. He loves the toasted cheese on bread that finishes the soup perfectly, so don't skip this part—it's scrumptious!

12 cups finely chopped sweet onions

3 tablespoons olive oil

3 tablespoons unsalted butter

6 cups extra strong beef broth

1 tablespoon sugar

1 teaspoon freshly ground black pepper

½ pound grated Swiss cheese

½ cup freshly grated Parmesan cheese

6 thin slices French bread, toasted

1) In a large pot or Dutch oven, place onions, olive oil, and butter. Cook over low heat until onions have softened, stirring often.

2) Add broth, sugar, and black pepper, stirring to blend. Bring soup to a slow boil, reduce heat to low, and simmer at least 30 minutes. Keep warm until ready to serve.

3) In a small bowl, mix cheeses, and set aside. Trim bread slices to fit into bowls or ramekins that can go into the oven and under broiler. Preheat oven to 350°, and raise oven rack close to broiling unit. Place bowls on heavy cookie sheet for stability.

4) Fill 6 bowls with soup, leaving room for bread. Place 1 slice of bread in each bowl, and sprinkle with cheese mixture.

5) Bake 10–15 minutes, then lightly brown cheese under broiler. Serve hot.

Mississippi Seafood Chowder

SERVES 4–6.

We love this thick, rich soup served with hot rolls or toasted French bread right out of the oven. In New England, chowder is always served with oyster crackers, but in the South, we love our hot breads, especially with good soup!

4 fish fillets (catfish, tilapia, cod, snapper, etc.)

½ pound small or medium shrimp, shelled, tail off

4 cups diced potatoes

4 cups diced onions

¼ teaspoon ground thyme

1 teaspoon salt

½ teaspoon coarsely ground black pepper

1 cup milk

1 cup heavy cream

½ cup unsalted butter

1) Place fish and shrimp in large pan, and cover completely with water. Bring water to a simmer, and cook fish about 15 minutes, until fish flakes. Remove fish and shrimp from broth with a slotted spoon, transfer to a bowl, and set aside.

2) To broth, add potatoes, onions, thyme, salt, and black pepper, stirring well. Simmer about 30 minutes, until vegetables are cooked. Stir in milk, cream, and butter.

3) Return fish and shrimp to pot, and stir gently. Simmer another 2 minutes; taste, and adjust seasonings, if needed. Serve warm.

4) The chowder can be refrigerated at this point for 1–2 days, or frozen, then heated very gently.

Broccoli and Mushroom Soup

SERVES 6–8.

Our rich and creamy broccoli soup is always on the menu at The Crown. Fresh broccoli makes such a difference in texture and flavor, but canned mushrooms will work fine, too. If you don't have Swiss cheese, Cheddar cheese subs nicely. Make the soup your own so your family will enjoy it as much as our guests at The Crown do!

SOUPS

2 sticks unsalted butter

1 small onion, diced

8 ounces fresh mushrooms, sliced thinly

4 cups diced fresh broccoli

1 cup all-purpose flour

4–5 cups milk, divided

1 cup chicken broth

1 cup grated Swiss cheese

1 teaspoon salt

1 teaspoon coarsely ground black pepper

1) Melt butter in large saucepan or Dutch oven on medium heat. Add onion, mushrooms, and broccoli, tossing and stirring vegetables in butter 2–3 minutes. Sprinkle flour into pan, continuing to stir so flour is evenly distributed and mixed with vegetables, and flour is being cooked—you are making a roux for this thick nourishing soup, so stir for another 2 minutes to blend completely.

2) Add 3 cups milk, continuing to stir vigorously to create a sauce. Turn heat to low, and continue stirring. As soup thickens, add chicken broth and additional milk, a little at a time, stirring constantly so soup stays smooth. Cook another 2 minutes, stirring constantly.

3) Add cheese, salt, and black pepper, stirring while cheese melts. Add more milk if you want a thinner soup.

4) Cool, and refrigerate until needed. Soup keeps well 2–3 days, but may need a touch more milk when reheating.

Broccoli and Mushroom Soup

CREAMY DELTA BISQUE

SERVES 6.

This rich creamy soup was featured on Turner South's Blue Ribbon TV show when the crew came to film at The Crown in Indianola. We enjoy it often at home and usually eat it once as a soup, and the next day, we add Parmesan cheese and serve it over pasta. That makes a royal leftover or "bonus meal," as I like to say!

4 U.S. Farm-Raised Catfish fillets

1 stick plus 2 tablespoons unsalted butter, divided

4 green onions, sliced

2 stalks celery, finely chopped

⅓ cup all-purpose flour

4 cups milk

1 cup heavy cream

1 teaspoon Tabasco

1 tablespoon chopped parsley

1 bay leaf

1 tablespoon chopped chives

1 teaspoon salt

1) Cut catfish into 1-inch pieces. Place 2 tablespoons butter in large saucepan; add catfish, onions, and celery, and simmer slowly 3–4 minutes, but do not brown. Transfer to a bowl, and set aside.

2) In same pan, melt remaining 1 stick butter over medium heat; add flour, and stir 2–3 minutes to keep roux smooth. Do not brown.

3) Slowly add milk and cream, continuing to stir while bisque thickens.

4) Return catfish mixture to pan, and add Tabasco, parsley, bay leaf, chives, and salt, stirring gently. Simmer very slowly, 10–15 minutes.

5) Serve immediately, or bisque can be refrigerated for up to 3 days.

TIDBIT: Catfish is a big Mississippi Delta farming crop, and we have always promoted it on our menu at The Crown. In 1993, our *Classic Catfish* cookbook was published with 110 recipes using catfish, in ways other than fried. I developed Catfish Bisque for that cookbook from a shrimp bisque recipe I've been using for a long time. You can easily prepare it using shrimp. Simply substitute peeled shrimp for the catfish, and carry on. For crab bisque, just add crabmeat at the end, and let it simmer a bit.

THE CROWN'S CHICKEN AND SAUSAGE GUMBO

MAKES 3 QUARTS.

Gumbo is one of our most popular menu items at The Crown. Lots of guests get a cup as their appetizer, and Tony has a bowl almost every day, because "it's so satisfying." We think the "heat" is just right, but some ask for Tabasco, and heat it a lot more.

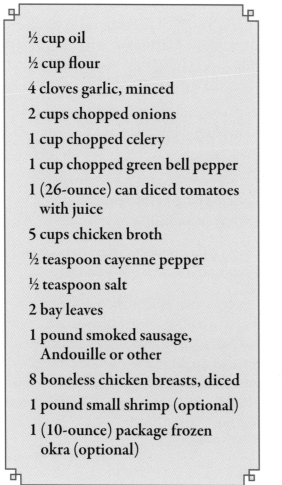

½ cup oil

½ cup flour

4 cloves garlic, minced

2 cups chopped onions

1 cup chopped celery

1 cup chopped green bell pepper

1 (26-ounce) can diced tomatoes with juice

5 cups chicken broth

½ teaspoon cayenne pepper

½ teaspoon salt

2 bay leaves

1 pound smoked sausage, Andouille or other

8 boneless chicken breasts, diced

1 pound small shrimp (optional)

1 (10-ounce) package frozen okra (optional)

1) In a large, heavy stockpot, heat oil on medium heat; stir in flour to make a roux. Cook, stirring constantly, over medium heat about 30 minutes, until it is a rich, milk chocolate color.

2) When the roux is just right, add garlic, onions, celery, and bell pepper, and stir vigorously. Cook 2 minutes, turn heat to low, and simmer 15 minutes, stirring occasionally.

3) Add tomatoes, broth, cayenne, salt, bay leaves, sausage, chicken, and shrimp (and okra, if you choose), and simmer 1 hour or more, stirring occasionally. Taste, and add salt and cayenne pepper, as desired, or Tabasco, if you like it hot. Serve hot with a little cooked rice sitting on top.

TIDBIT: In Louisiana, whatever they have is what goes into their gumbo—and it's always good. Add any fish you like, or try duck or venison. Down in south Louisiana, they serve cold potato salad with gumbo, to cool our mouth from the spice in the gumbo, we were told. Of course, we tried it because I'm always ready to try something new. Good!

Belgian Beer Beef Stew

SERVES 4–6.

Rich, dark flavor fills this wonderful Belgian stew that we enjoy often at home served over boiled potatoes to capture all the delicious gravy on the plate. So different and so good!

2 pounds boneless beef (such as chuck roast)

1 cup flour

½ teaspoon salt

½ teaspoon coarsely ground black pepper

Pinch of thyme

½ stick unsalted butter, divided

1 onion, thinly sliced

1 clove garlic, minced

1 (12-ounce) bottle dark beer (Belgian is good)

½ teaspoon sugar

½ teaspoon vinegar

1) Cut meat into 1½-inch cubes. In a bowl. combine flour, salt, black pepper, and thyme. Toss meat pieces in seasoned flour.

2) In heavy Dutch oven on medium heat, melt 1 tablespoon butter. Add onion and garlic, and sauté lightly, then transfer to a large bowl.

3) In same pan, add 2 tablespoons butter and half the coated meat cubes, tossing repeatedly to lightly brown on all sides. Transfer browned meat to onion bowl. Add remaining 1 tablespoon butter, and brown remaining meat.

4) Remove pan from heat. Return meat and onions to the Dutch oven, and set aside.

5) In a saucepan, combine beer and sugar, bring to a boil, and pour immediately over meat; stir to combine. Cover, return to heat, and simmer slowly about 2 hours. Taste, and adjust seasoning as desired. Stir in vinegar, and serve hot over boiled new potatoes.

TIDBIT: Beef Carbonnade Flamande is the Belgian name for this delicious beef stew that we tasted in Brussels, and have enjoyed cooking ever since. We spent four days in Brussels, and ate our way through the old quarter, trying everything and loving it all.

THE FAMILY CAMP STEW

MAKES 5 GALLONS.

Yes, I know this recipe will feed an army, but a very happy one! So unless you are cooking for a crowd, you'll want to freeze some of the stew, and it freezes perfectly. Cut the recipe down if you want to, but do try this old southern camp stew. Invite some friends and neighbors over to enjoy it with you—that's southern hospitality.

4 pounds chicken, cooked, boned, and cut in small pieces

4 pounds pork roast, chopped into small pieces

4 pounds beef roast, chopped into small pieces

3 (15-ounce) cans creamed corn

2 (15-ounce) cans whole-kernel corn

4 (26-ounce) cans diced tomatoes

1 (32-ounce) package frozen butter beans

3 pounds onions, chopped

5 pounds potatoes, chopped large

1 (32-ounce) bottle ketchup

½ cup prepared mustard

1 cup sugar

1 (4-ounce) bottle Louisiana Hot Sauce

1 (32-ounce) package frozen okra (optional)

1) In a huge stockpot, place all the ingredients, and mix well. Add water to cover ingredients, and stir thoroughly.

2) Cover, and cook on medium heat 6 hours, stirring very frequently, and adding water as needed. Keep stirring, because it can scorch easily, if not stirred well.

3) If you choose to add okra, add it during last 2 hours of cooking. Just keep stirring!

TIDBIT: This recipe is my brother-in-law Larry's combination of two recipes—one from my mama and one from Larry's daddy. Over the years, Larry has added and subtracted from both recipes, and created what is now Larry's special recipe for the Family Camp Stew (or PePaw's Camp Stew, as his grandchildren call it). Of course, being the BBQ cook Larry is, he makes sure that some of the meat in his stew has been on the grill and smoked. He smokes a roast, serves some, then puts the rest in the freezer to save for the stew that he's planning. You don't have to smoke the meat, but it does add another depth of flavor. It's a big recipe, but you'll be so happy you have some in the freezer to enjoy!

RED BEAN AND CATFISH CHILI

SERVES 4.

Catfish chili was in our 1992 Classic Catfish cookbook and was my favorite recipe to cook during a book signing. The smell of the spices simmering is incredible, and the chili served a lot of "bites" to hungry cookbook lovers who came into the store following the aromas! It's totally delicious with the bonus of being a truly healthy meal!

1 tablespoon olive oil

1 large onion, diced

1 large green bell pepper, diced

3 cloves garlic, minced, or 1 teaspoon garlic powder

2 tablespoons chili powder

1 teaspoon cinnamon

1 teaspoon oregano

½ teaspoon salt

1 (15-ounce) can diced tomatoes

1 (15-ounce) can kidney beans, drained and rinsed

4 raw catfish fillets, diced

1) Put olive oil in large saucepan over medium heat.

2) Add onion, bell pepper, garlic, chili powder, cinnamon, oregano, and salt. Cook over medium heat a few minutes, stirring constantly. (The aroma is wonderful!)

3) Add tomatoes and beans, and stir well.

4) Place catfish on top, and stir gently into hot chili. Reduce heat to low, and simmer at least 15 minutes.

5) Serve in a bowl with crackers, or over rice as a main dish.

Captain Catfish with Jill Cordes from Food Network (left) and his biggest fans, Evelyn (center) and Tony at the Belzoni Catfish Festival.

SALADS

The Crown's Fresh Spinach Salad

THE FAMILY CHRISTMAS SALAD

SERVES 12–15.

So scrumptious...it's almost a dessert, and perfect with that turkey sandwich for supper!

1 (6-ounce) box black cherry Jell-O

2 cups boiling water

1 (21-ounce) can cherry pie filling

1 (16-ounce) can crushed pineapple

1 (8-ounce) container Cool Whip

1 (14-ounce) can sweetened condensed milk

½ cup chopped pecans

1) Place Jell-O in bowl, add boiling water, and stir to dissolve. Allow mixture to cool.

2) Pour pie filling into bowl, then cut cherries into halves or smaller pieces. Add pie filling and pineapple to cooled Jell-O, and mix well.

3) In large bowl, thoroughly mix Cool Whip and sweetened condensed milk. Stir in pecans, then add cooled Jell-O mixture, and combine well.

4) Pour into 9x13-inch pan, and refrigerate until thickened and chilled.

TIP: May use strawberry Jell-O, and 2 (10-ounce) boxes frozen strawberries to substitute for the pie filling and pineapple.

TIDBIT: Congealed salads are an integral part of southern festive meals, at home or at church suppers. Holidays are always potluck at our house, with all the cousins and friends who come contributing a dish or two. The buffet table would be incomplete without several deliciously cold, fruit-filled congealed salads. I always count on Phil and Dell McDade for the yummy congealed salads they make and bring to family gatherings. And they always leave me the leftovers!

SALADS

CREAMY MANDARIN SALAD

SERVES 12–15.

So simple to prepare, tastes luscious, and holds well for several days. I love eating it for dessert.

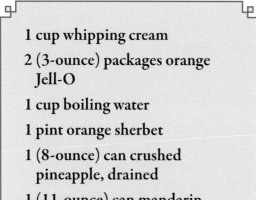

1 cup whipping cream

2 (3-ounce) packages orange Jell-O

1 cup boiling water

1 pint orange sherbet

1 (8-ounce) can crushed pineapple, drained

1 (11-ounce) can mandarin oranges, drained

1 cup miniature marshmallows

1) Beat whipping cream, and set aside.

2) In a large bowl, dissolve Jell-O in boiling water, mixing well.

3) Add sherbet to Jell-O, and stir rapidly until dissolved, and mixture is thickened.

4) Add pineapple, oranges, and marshmallows to mixture, stirring well.

5) Fold in whipped cream gently but completely.

6) Pour into 9x13-inch pan, and chill in refrigerator until ready to serve.

STRAWBERRY NUT SALAD

SERVES 12–15.

Try this tangy-sweet layered salad, because it looks so pretty and is absolutely delicious! You might be tempted to eat it for dessert.

2 (3-ounce) packages strawberry Jell-O

1 cup boiling water

2 (10-ounce) boxes frozen strawberries, thawed

1 (20-ounce) can crushed pineapple, drained

1 cup chopped pecans

1 pint sour cream

1) In a large bowl, dissolve Jell-O in boiling water, mixing well.

2) Add strawberries, pineapple, and pecans, combining thoroughly.

3) Spread half the mixture in a 9x13-inch pan, spreading fruit evenly. Refrigerate about an hour to thicken.

4) Leave remaining half of mixture at room temperature until first is congealed.

5) Spread sour cream very gently over congealed layer, then spoon remaining salad mixture carefully over sour cream. Put back in refrigerator until firm.

6) Serve on lettuce leaves with a dab of sour cream, if desired.

CRANBERRY CREAM CHEESE SALAD

SERVES 12–15.

2 (3-ounce) packages cranberry Jell-O (or any red Jell-O)

1½ cups boiling water

1½ cups cold water

½ teaspoon cinnamon

1 medium apple, peeled and chopped finely

1 (15-ounce) can whole cranberry sauce

1 (8-ounce) package cream cheese, softened

1) Place Jell-O in medium bowl. Add boiling water, and stir until dissolved. Add cold water and cinnamon, and stir well.

2) Pour 2 cups Jell-O mixture into large bowl, and refrigerate about 1½ hours, until thickened. Reserve remaining Jell-O at room temperature.

3) Stir apple and cranberry sauce into chilled Jell-O, and pour into 9x13-inch pan, then refrigerate again.

4) In small bowl, stir cream cheese until smooth. Add reserved room temperature Jell-O to cream cheese, and mix until smooth.

5) Spoon cream cheese mixture over congealed layer in pan, carefully smoothing it evenly to form a topping. Cover, and refrigerate until ready to serve.

TIDBIT: This was one of my favorite congealed fruit salads to serve at bridge parties. We even made a special bridge area in the middle of the antique furniture at the shop, so the ladies could be served dessert there. Bridge luncheons and dessert parties still take place at The Crown, with groups coming from across the Delta to play bridge and enjoy our food. We don't have a special place to play any longer, but tables are scattered throughout the gift shop, tucked into the book corner and the classic toy section when the bridge clubs come to lunch.

SALADS

WORLD'S BEST CATFISH SALAD

SERVES 6–8.

That's what Delta Magazine called it in an article, and our customers agree! They featured our "World's Best Catfish Salad" in one of their stories about cooking catfish in unusual ways, which has been a mission of ours at The Crown since 1980 when farm-raised catfish was a big crop in the Mississippi Delta.

8 U.S. Farm-Raised Catfish fillets

½ teaspoon Old Bay Seasoning or crab boil

1 lemon, sliced

4 cups water

1 cup mayonnaise

½ cup finely chopped celery

Juice of half a lemon

½ teaspoon salt

½ teaspoon coarsely ground black pepper

1) Cut catfish into bite-size pieces. Place in a saucepan with Old Bay Seasoning, sliced lemon, and water. Bring water barely to a boil, cut off heat, and let catfish cool in the seasoned water.

2) Drain well; mix gently with mayonnaise and celery. Taste, and adjust seasonings as desired, adding lemon juice, salt, and black pepper. Refrigerate until ready to serve.

3) Serve a scoop on top of a quartered tomato, in the old-fashioned way, or as a healthy and delicious sandwich.

TIP: Use this recipe with any fresh fish to create your own fresh, unprocessed fish salad.

The Crown's Chicken Salad

SERVES 6–8.

We serve and sell gallons of our chicken salad every week, and it's made fresh every day. It is perfect for a sandwich, or to eat with crackers.

6–8 bone-in chicken breasts (or boneless)

1 teaspoon salt

½ teaspoon garlic powder

1 teaspoon coarsely ground black pepper

5 celery stalks, finely chopped

1 cup mayonnaise

Juice of half a lemon

1) Wash chicken breasts , and place in large saucepan. Sprinkle with salt, garlic powder, and black pepper, and add enough water to barely cover chicken. Bring to a boil, and immediately turn heat to low; simmer until done. Do not overcook! Remove chicken to cutting board, and reserve broth to strain and use later.

2) Debone chicken, and cut into small pieces. Place chicken pieces in large mixing bowl.

3) Add celery, mayonnaise, and lemon juice, and mix thoroughly so chicken shreds just a little bit as you stir. Keeps in refrigerator 2–3 days.

TIDBIT: Our Chicken Salad Plate at The Crown has two scoops of chicken salad served with a bed of mixed greens topped with chopped apples, cantaloupe, Crispy Crumbles (page 80), and Vidalia dressing, plus a scoop of another of our vegetable salads— whatever we decide we are hungry for, and want to serve that day. It's a delicious plate, and a great favorite with our guests.

My Favorite Green Bean Salad

SERVES 20.

Enjoy this recipe as a salad or a vegetable. It will hold two weeks refrigerated, and just gets better the longer it sits.

1 cup oil

1⅔ cups white vinegar

1½ cups sugar

2 teaspoons salt

1 teaspoon black pepper

1 medium onion, sliced

1 large green bell pepper, sliced

2 (24-ounce) cans green beans

2 (15-ounce) cans red kidney beans

1) Combine oil, vinegar, sugar, salt, and black pepper in large bowl, mixing well to dissolve sugar.

2) Stir in onion and bell pepper.

3) Drain and rinse thoroughly all beans, then add to mixture, stirring gently together. Refrigerate until needed.

TIDBIT: This is one of the recipes I found in a cookbook while we were in Thailand. The library there was filled with cookbooks, even though the airmen had no place to cook a thing. I studied them all. I could find all the ingredients in the local market, so this became a standard salad at our house in Ubon...and later on the salad bar at The Crown. I love a salad that holds well, and that can be made ahead to feed a crowd. And I do love feeding a crowd!

Tangy Cucumber and Onions

SERVES 4–6.

A forever favorite at our house! This salad is a nice side dish with roasted meats. The tart juices mix well with meat on the plate. I like to serve it when we have barbecue with baked beans and potato salad, instead of coleslaw.

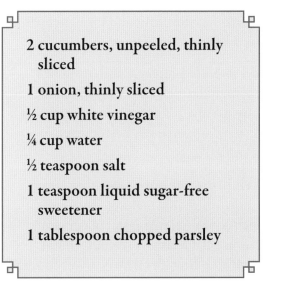

2 cucumbers, unpeeled, thinly sliced

1 onion, thinly sliced

½ cup white vinegar

¼ cup water

½ teaspoon salt

1 teaspoon liquid sugar-free sweetener

1 tablespoon chopped parsley

1) Place cucumbers and onion in a large glass bowl.

2) Add remaining ingredients, and mix thoroughly.

3) Delicious immediately, but even better chilled several hours before serving. Will hold refrigerated for several days. So great for a party!

TIDBIT: I like to serve my cucumbers (and a lot of other vegetables) unpeeled. I like the green color of the cucumber slices in this dish. The skins of most vegetables and fruits are also good for you, and I see no reason to peel them. Be sure to rinse and scrub well. My aunt and grandmother always peeled their tomatoes, but Mama did not, and neither do I.

SALADS

73

MAMA'S MARINATED COLESLAW

SERVES 10–12.

This tangy fresh-tasting coleslaw makes a lot of my guests at The Crown happy, because it's marinated with no mayonnaise. Taste in coleslaw is very personal, and I like Mama's.

SALADS

1 cup vinegar

¾ cup sugar

½ cup water

½ cup oil

1 onion, finely diced

1 teaspoon salt

1 teaspoon coarsely ground black pepper

1 head cabbage, shredded, or 2 bags prepared slaw

1 green bell pepper, finely diced, (optional)

1) In a large bowl, combine vinegar, sugar, water, oil, onion, salt, and black pepper. Mix well to dissolve sugar thoroughly.

2) Add shredded cabbage and diced bell pepper, if desired, and refrigerate until ready to serve. You can serve immediately, but the slaw gets even better when it sits for several days.

TIDBIT: This is the only slaw that I ever remember my mama making. Mama was a home economics major in college, and worked in the Delta as a traveling home economist, calling on farmers' wives to teach them how to can and preserve foods. I don't know where this recipe originated, but my guess is it came from those experiences of making fresh food last. When the slaw sits for a week, it's almost like fresh sauerkraut, and tastes wonderful!

THE CROWN'S
FRESH SPINACH SALAD

SERVES 4. MAKES 2 CUPS DRESSING.

You'll love the dressing for this salad...sweet and tangy, and it only takes a little to get lots of flavor on this healthy salad. Delicious on any type of salad.

TANGY TOMATO DRESSING:

½ cup diced onion

⅓ cup white vinegar

⅓ cup ketchup

2 tablespoons Worcestershire

½ teaspoon salt

¾ cup sugar

1 cup oil

SALAD:

1 large package fresh spinach

4 ounces fresh mushrooms, sliced

1 (8-ounce) can mandarin oranges, drained

Toasted almonds to garnish, optional

1) For dressing, blend onion, vinegar, ketchup, Worcestershire, and salt for 1 minute.

2) With blender running, slowly sprinkle in sugar. Then very slowly pour in oil so that it emulsifies, and dressing is smooth. Keep blender running for 1 minute.

3) Dressing will keep in a covered container refrigerated for a week.

4) Just before serving, prepare salad by tossing spinach in large bowl with just enough dressing to lightly coat spinach leaves.

5) Toss again with mushrooms and most of the oranges, reserving a few to garnish top of salad. Sprinkle almonds on top to garnish.

TIP: I also like to use this as the dressing in Mama's Meatloaf, and drizzled over a fresh citrus salad of grapefruit and oranges.

FRESH VEGETABLE VINAIGRETTE

MAKES 1½ CUPS.

I like to marinate each vegetable separately, so that decorating the serving tray is easier. Arrange vegetables in swirls on a big tray, alternating colors and using as many vegetables as you like. I love button mushrooms, asparagus, Roma tomatoes, zucchini, yellow squash, green beans, cucumbers, and bell peppers. Choose the freshest you can find!

1 cup vegetable or olive oil

⅓ cup white vinegar

1 teaspoon oregano leaves

1 teaspoon salt

½ teaspoon coarsely ground black pepper

½ teaspoon dry mustard

1 clove garlic, crushed and minced

2 tablespoons finely minced onion

2 tablespoons minced parsley

1) Combine all ingredients in a lidded jar, and shake well to blend.

2) Drizzle vinaigrette over vegetables, turning gently to coat each side. Refrigerate a least 3 hours, or up to 24 hours.

NOTE: This recipe will marinate enough vegetables to serve 15–20. Simply double or triple the vinaigrette if you are serving a larger crowd.

To prepare vegetables before marinating:

- Button mushrooms: whole
- Cucumbers: sliced, or in spears
- Cherry tomatoes: whole
- Roma tomatoes: sliced
- Zucchini and yellow squash: sliced, or in spears
- Bell peppers: cored carefully, then cut into spears
- Green beans, whole: Cut ends, and place in boiling water. Return to boil, leave beans for 1 minute, then remove to icy water to cool. Drain.
- Asparagus: Discard lower stem by bending each until it breaks, then place in boiling water. Return to boil, then remove to icy water to cool. Drain.

TIDBIT: The vinaigrette-marinated vegetables are wonderful on a sideboard for a large dinner party or cocktail buffet. Vegetables are fresh, but don't need a dip to make them delicious. The vegetables and vinaigrette have been beautiful at wedding receptions, rehearsal parties, and events of all sizes. Plus, if all the vegetables are not served, they still taste wonderful for several days.

Fresh Vegetable Vinaigrette

77

POPPY SEED DRESSING

MAKES 1 QUART.

Perfect to drizzle over fresh fruit, or toss with a green salad. Mix dressing with Cool Whip to top congealed salads as a garnish. Try the dressing as a dip for fresh strawberries or fruit kebabs.

⅔ cup vinegar

2 teaspoons dry mustard

2 teaspoons salt

½ small white onion, cut in 3 pieces

1½ cups sugar

2 cups oil

3 tablespoons poppy seeds or celery seeds

1) Blend vinegar, mustard, salt, and onion for 1 minute.

2) With blender running, very slowly add sugar, a little at a time, to dissolve. Blend for 1 minute after sugar is dissolved.

3) Then with blender still running, very slowly add oil so that it can emulsify well. Keep running for another minute, then add poppy seeds; stop when seeds are thoroughly mixed.

4) Pour into a jar, and refrigerate up to 2 weeks. Shake well before using.

Buttermilk Salad Dressing

MAKES 3 CUPS.

This is an old southern recipe like a homemade "ranch" dressing, but better. My grandmother used it on her "combination" salad. Now we use it as a dip for chicken tenders, fresh vegetables, and everything else that can be dipped.

1 cup buttermilk

2 cups mayonnaise

¼ cup chopped white or green onion

½ teaspoon garlic powder

½ teaspoon The Crown's Sassy Seasoning (page 218) or seasoned salt

¼ teaspoon coarsely ground black pepper

2 tablespoons dried parsley

1) Place buttermilk and mayonnaise in bowl of electric mixer. Beat 1 minute on low; add onion, and beat again.

2) Add garlic powder, Sassy Seasoning, black pepper, and parsley, and beat 1 more minute.

3) Pour into jar, and refrigerate. Keeps well refrigerated for 1 week.

VARIATION: To make Chipotle Ranch Dressing, add just a bit of chipotle sauce to this basic recipe, to give it a kick. May use Tabasco, but we do like the smoky chipotle.

Indianola is the county seat of Sunflower County where we grow sunflowers in fields and yards. It is the Delta's signature flower arrangement for homes and churches.

SALADS

79

CRISPY CRUMBLES

MAKES 4 CUPS.

These crumbles are tiny little bursts of flavor that enhance every bite of our green salads at The Crown, and our customers love them. They are the crowning glory of most any salad.

½ stick unsalted butter

2 teaspoons The Crown's Sassy Seasoning (page 218) or seasoned salt

1 teaspoon or more garlic powder

2 tablespoons paprika

6 cups crumbled bread or rolls (very small pieces)

1) Melt butter in small saucepan; add Sassy Seasoning, garlic powder, and paprika, and mix well.

2) Spread bread crumbs evenly in 9x13-inch (or larger) baking pan. Drizzle butter mixture over bread crumbs, stirring well to season evenly.

3) Bake about 1 hour in preheated 250° oven, stirring every 15 minutes, until all crumbs are well coated and beginning to dry out. Turn off oven, and leave crumbs in oven to cool.

4) Store in tightly closed container. Will keep at room temperature 2–3 weeks.

TIDBIT: Customers ask us about these crumbles every day, and buy them to take home. They are not your normal croutons, but you can use them that way as well. I use them to bread chicken breasts that we are going to simply bake in the oven. Crumbles give Chicken Kiev (page 122) extra flavor, and can perk up a simple green salad on a busy night. They are always in the pantry at our house, and we've served them at The Crown since 1976.

Vegetables & Sides

Crisp Zucchini Sauté

Fried Lady Fingers
(Whole pods of okra)

SERVES 4.

We love our fried foods in the South. Fried vegetables are a good example. After all, it is a vegetable, and vegetables are good for us, right? I've been frying whole pods of okra for a long time. I love it this way, and it doesn't absorb as much fat, so it must be healthy!

25 small okra pods (or more)

2 eggs

½ cup all-purpose flour

½ cup cornmeal (or more flour)

1 teaspoon The Crown's Sassy Seasoning (page 218) or seasoned salt

Oil for frying

Tip: Eggplant can be cooked exactly the same way. Cut unpeeled eggplant the size of index finger. Batter and cook exactly the same, but when they come out of the hot oil, sprinkle with Parmesan cheese, and serve hot. Commander's Palace in New Orleans served these years ago when guests first sat down at the table and were studying the menu. We borrowed that idea, and have been cooking them ever since.

1) Choose the smallest pods of fresh okra you can find. Wash and pat dry, but don't cut off any of the pod; leave the "cap" intact.

2) Beat eggs in a small bowl. In a larger separate bowl, combine flour, cornmeal, and Sassy Seasoning. Dip each okra pod in flour mixture, then in eggs, then back in flour mixture, and set aside on cookie sheet to "dry." Continue dipping okra until all are battered.

3) Add oil to heavy frying pan to 1½-inch depth, and heat on medium high. When oil is hot, add 6–8 okra to hot oil, but do not crowd. When okra is lightly brown, remove from oil, drain, and add more okra. They cook very quickly. Serve hot as a vegetable or a pickup appetizer.

MARINATED FRESH ASPARAGUS

SERVES 10–12.

Asparagus is a wonderful side dish with richly sauced meats or fish, or on a chicken salad plate. It keeps color best if used within twenty-four hours, but still delicious after three days.

1 cup oil

⅓ cup white vinegar

1 teaspoons oregano leaves

1 teaspoon salt

½ teaspoon coarsely ground black pepper

½ teaspoon dry mustard

1 clove garlic, crushed and minced

2 tablespoons finely minced onion

2 tablespoons finely minced parsley

2 pounds fresh asparagus

1) Combine oil, vinegar, oregano, salt, black pepper, mustard, garlic, onion, and parsley in a jar with a lid, and shake well to blend. Set aside.

2) Discard lower stem of asparagus by bending each one individually until it breaks, leaving the tender part. (Reserve lower stems to peel and slice into sticks for dips or just snacking.)

3) In large pot or Dutch oven, bring 2 quarts water to a boil. Place asparagus into boiling water just long enough for water to come back to a boil. Immediately lift asparagus from water, and place in bowl of ice water to cool. Drain asparagus on cookie sheet, then place in glass bowl or baking dish.

4) Drizzle asparagus with vinaigrette, turning gently to coat each side. Cover, and refrigerate until ready to serve. Holds well for 3 days.

TIDBIT: Asparagus is an elegant vegetable, and we love this cold version. Try hot asparagus with butter, cooked the same way, just lifted out hot and straight into a serving dish. Dot with butter and a pinch of salt, turning to coat well. A squeeze of lemon is always good. We use only the small spears of asparagus.

ROASTED ASPARAGUS WITH PEPPERS AND ONION

SERVES 4–6.

Asparagus taste delicious, and are so healthy, roasted with just a drizzle of olive oil and salt. I love the sweetness of the roasted onion and bell peppers.

1 pound fresh asparagus, pencil thin

1 small red bell pepper

1 small yellow bell pepper

1 small green bell pepper

1 medium white onion

Olive oil to drizzle

Salt to sprinkle

1) Discard lower stem of asparagus by bending each stalk until it breaks, leaving the tender part. Set aside. Seed bell peppers, and cut into 1-inch strips. Peel onion, trim ends, and cut into 8 wedges.

2) Spread bell peppers and onion out on large cookie sheet with sides. Drizzle a little olive oil over vegetables, turning to coat well. Sprinkle with salt, and roast in preheated 450° oven 10 minutes, turning vegetables after 5 minutes.

3) Remove from oven, move vegetables over to edges, and add asparagus to middle of pan. Drizzle asparagus with a little olive oil and salt, and return to oven 10 more minutes, turning all vegetables after 5 minutes. Serve hot or cold.

TIDBIT: When I serve roast pork or chicken, I like to roast vegetables to enjoy with it. The vegetables will cook in the same hot oven. Prepare your vegetables completely, and pop them in the oven a few minutes before the roast is finished—just remember that new potatoes need an extra 10 minutes before you add the more tender vegetables. Stir vegetables when you take the roast out; they will finish cooking while your roast rests, and dinner will be ready to serve, hot and delicious.

SIDE DISHES

*Roasted Asparagus with
Peppers and Onion*

THE CROWN'S BLACK BUTTER GREEN BEANS

SERVES 4.

We get questions daily from our guests about our green beans, and how to make them. I love sharing this recipe, and always emphasize that you can use the butter on anything to give it that piquant flavor!

1–2 tablespoons Black Butter (page 215)

½ cup sesame seeds

1 (15-ounce) can whole green beans (we use Blue Lake)

1) Warm Black Butter slightly in a stainless pan, add sesame seeds, and stir for a few seconds. Do NOT let seeds burn.

2) Heat beans in separate saucepan. Completely drain hot beans (so butter won't get watered down), and stir in Black Butter; serve immediately.

CRISP ZUCCHINI SAUTÉ

SERVES 4.

This quick method captures the fresh flavor of the vegetables. I especially love it in the summer when I can pick the smallest squash and zucchini to slice.

1–2 tablespoons unsalted butter

1 cup thinly sliced zucchini

1 cup thinly sliced yellow squash

¼ cup grated carrots (optional)

¼ teaspoon Italian seasoning

¼ teaspoon salt

1) Melt butter in skillet on medium heat. Add zucchini, squash, and carrots, and cook until just barely done, 2–3 minutes, turning constantly to coat with butter.

2) Sprinkle with Italian seasoning and salt. This sauté doesn't hold really well, so be sure it is the last thing you prepare before serving the meal.

SIDE DISHES

RATATOUILLE DELTA STYLE

SERVES 8–10.

This flavorful Mediterranean dish is wonderful served with grilled chicken, pork chops, or steak, made the day before serving, and lightly heated, or even served cold. Especially delicious when all these fresh vegetables are available at the local farmer's market. When we were in the cotton fields, Ratatouille Delta Style was a favorite served with our Chicken Kiev (page 122) on a rice pilaf—fresh, colorful, a little different, and always enjoyed.

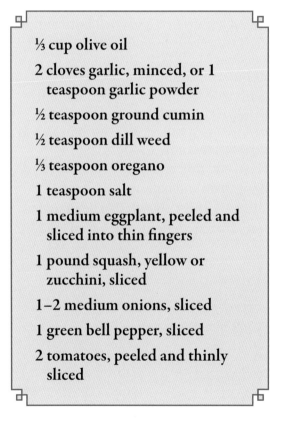

⅓ cup olive oil

2 cloves garlic, minced, or 1 teaspoon garlic powder

½ teaspoon ground cumin

½ teaspoon dill weed

⅓ teaspoon oregano

1 teaspoon salt

1 medium eggplant, peeled and sliced into thin fingers

1 pound squash, yellow or zucchini, sliced

1–2 medium onions, sliced

1 green bell pepper, sliced

2 tomatoes, peeled and thinly sliced

1) In small bowl or measuring cup, whisk together oil, garlic, cumin, dill, oregano, and salt, and set aside.

2) Butter a 9x13-inch baking dish. Layer vegetables in dish, starting with eggplant, scattering vegetables evenly across dish. Continue layering until vegetables are used.

3) Whisk oil and spices again. Drizzle mixture evenly over vegetables. Cover, and bake in preheated 350° oven 1 hour.

4) Serve immediately, or set aside uncovered, and reheat gently when ready to serve.

OLD-FASHIONED SQUASH CASSEROLE

SERVES 4–6.

Recipes using squash abound, but none is better than my grandmother's old-fashioned casserole that everyone in the family makes and enjoys when fresh squash is in season.

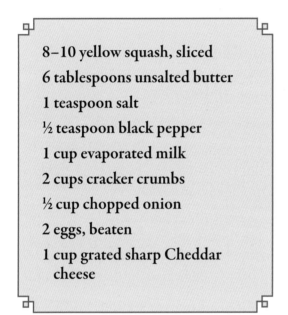

8–10 yellow squash, sliced

6 tablespoons unsalted butter

1 teaspoon salt

½ teaspoon black pepper

1 cup evaporated milk

2 cups cracker crumbs

½ cup chopped onion

2 eggs, beaten

1 cup grated sharp Cheddar cheese

1) Put squash in a large saucepan barely covered with water, and cook until almost soft. Drain well, and place in large bowl.

2) Cut butter into small pieces; add to hot squash with salt, black pepper, and milk, stirring well to melt butter.

3) Add cracker crumbs, onion, eggs, and cheese, and mix well. Pour into buttered baking dish, and bake at 350° for 40 minutes. (This casserole can be prepared ahead, frozen, thawed, and baked later.)

Sweet Corn Pudding

SERVES 10–12.

I love the texture of this traditional vegetable casserole that's almost like an egg custard, and just melts in your mouth. I guess that's why we call it a pudding.

4 eggs

1 (16-ounce) can whole-kernel corn, drained

1 (16-ounce) can cream-style corn

2 cups milk

½ stick unsalted butter

4 tablespoons sugar

2 green onions, thinly sliced

2 tablespoons cornstarch

½ teaspoon salt

1) In large bowl, beat eggs well with a fork. Add remaining ingredients, and mix thoroughly.

2) Pour corn mixture into buttered 9x13-inch baking dish. Bake in preheated 325° oven about 45 minutes, until light brown and firm.

3) Slice into squares to ensure nice, even servings. Pudding can be covered and kept warm for an hour before serving.

TIDBIT: This is one of my favorite vegetable dishes when we have special luncheons, and I cook it often at home. Really nice served with grilled chicken breasts, stuffed pork chops, or our Catfish Allison (page 142).

CORN FRITTERS

MAKES ABOUT 18.

Another yummy fried vegetable! These make nice appetizer bites, too!

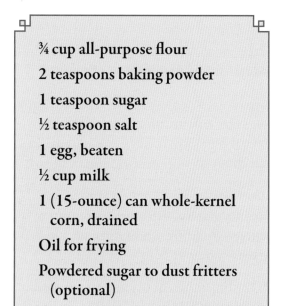

¾ cup all-purpose flour

2 teaspoons baking powder

1 teaspoon sugar

½ teaspoon salt

1 egg, beaten

½ cup milk

1 (15-ounce) can whole-kernel corn, drained

Oil for frying

Powdered sugar to dust fritters (optional)

1) Mix all ingredients together in one bowl. Heat oil in heavy frying pan, 1½ inches deep.

2) When oil is hot, drop fritter batter by level tablespoons in hot oil, turning as needed until browned. Do not crowd in pan.

3) Drain fritters, and dust with sugar, if desired.

CREAMY FRIED CORN

SERVES 6.

Fresh corn has always been enjoyed this way across the South. Tony's mama made it, and so did my family. It can only be made with fresh corn to get that juicy milk from it. This is a summertime treat!

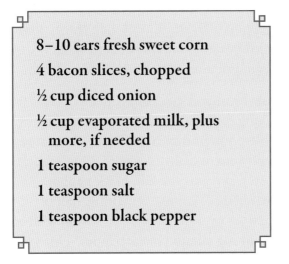

8–10 ears fresh sweet corn

4 bacon slices, chopped

½ cup diced onion

½ cup evaporated milk, plus more, if needed

1 teaspoon sugar

1 teaspoon salt

1 teaspoon black pepper

TIDBIT: Fried corn was always a treat when we were growing up. We usually ate corn on the cob, so much easier than the cutting and scraping needed for fried corn. Mama made this when the corn came in fresh, and she didn't fry bacon especially for it. She kept a container for bacon grease on the back of the stove, with a little strainer inside to catch stray bits as she poured it out of the hot skillet. We don't use bacon grease at our house to flavor peas and beans, but when I fry bacon for breakfast, I always save the grease and use it within a couple of days to cook mushrooms or onions and bell peppers. It *really* tastes good!

1) Shuck corn, removing silks carefully. (A vegetable brush helps a lot.) Using a sharp knife, working over a large bowl, cut kernels off cob, scraping knife down each ear to capture the sweet milky juice in the bowl. This should produce about 4 cups.

2) Cook bacon on medium heat in a large skillet until crisp. Remove bacon to paper towels to drain, but leave drippings in skillet.

3) Add onion and corn to skillet, and cook 2 minutes, stirring and scraping often. Reduce heat to low, and cook 5 more minutes or until corn is tender; add ½ cup evaporated milk, sugar, salt, and black pepper, and continue stirring as corn becomes creamy. Add more evaporated milk, as needed. Taste, and adjust seasonings as needed.

4) To serve, place in bowl, and top with bacon pieces.

91

CLASSIC FRENCH SCALLOPED POTATOES

SERVE 4–6.

This tastes so fresh and full of flavor. Julia Child's favorite potato dish...and mine, too!

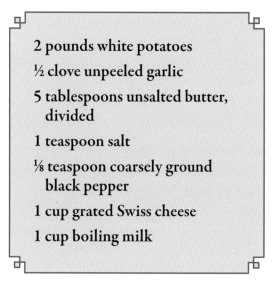

2 pounds white potatoes

½ clove unpeeled garlic

5 tablespoons unsalted butter, divided

1 teaspoon salt

⅛ teaspoon coarsely ground black pepper

1 cup grated Swiss cheese

1 cup boiling milk

1) Peel potatoes, and slice ⅛ inch thick. Place sliced potatoes in bowl of cold water. Drain potatoes, and dry well on a towel.

2) Rub 10-inch deep dish pie plate or similar baking dish with garlic, then smear with 1 tablespoon butter. Spread half of potatoes in bottom of dish. Dot with 2 tablespoons butter, and half the salt, black pepper, and cheese. Arrange remaining half of potatoes over first layer, and season with remaining salt and black pepper. Dot with remaining 2 tablespoons butter and cheese.

3) Bring milk to a boil in small saucepan, and pour evenly over potatoes. Bake in preheated 425° oven 20–30 minutes, or until potatoes are tender, milk has been absorbed, and top is nicely browned. Serve immediately, or cover and keep warm for up to an hour.

TIDBIT: My 1965 copy of Julia Child's *Mastering the Art of French Cooking* has so many pages splattered and wrinkled, that I was too embarrassed to take it to Natchez when we met her there. Julia did give me her autograph though, and it is framed, hanging in my dining room. I purchased new copies of her book for my children and grandchildren, and another one for me. But I always pick up my old spattered one; it's easier to find a recipe.

TIP: This recipe might be a little "last minute" for a dinner party, but the result is worth it. You can hold the sliced potatoes in water for several hours, prepare the baking dish, and have ingredients measured and ready to put together and run in the oven.

SIDE DISHES

*Classic French
Scalloped Potatoes*

French Cooking

GOURMET CHEESE GRITS

SERVES 4–6.

These fancy grits are wonderful served at a festive breakfast or with any great meal as a side dish. In the South, we love our grits anytime! I like to serve this recipe for a special breakfast or brunch with quiche, fresh fruit, and muffins.

2 cups half-and-half

2 cups milk

1 cup uncooked grits

1 stick unsalted butter, divided

1 teaspoon salt

½ teaspoon ground white pepper

2 eggs, beaten

4 ounces grated Gruyère, Swiss, or Cheddar cheese

½ cup freshly grated Parmesan cheese

1) Bring half-and-half and milk to a boil over medium heat, stirring often.

2) Add grits and ½ stick butter, and cook on medium heat, stirring until mixture is consistency of oatmeal, 3–5 minutes.

3) Remove grits from heat; whisk in salt, white pepper, and eggs until well combined.

4) Add remaining ½ stick butter and Gruyère cheese. Pour into buttered 2-quart casserole dish. Sprinkle with Parmesan, and bake in preheated 350° oven 1 hour. Serve immediately.

TIP: This recipe doubles perfectly to a 9x13-inch dish, and can be warmed successfully in the microwave the next day. The consistency won't be quite as creamy, but still delicious!

DELTA CHEESE GRITS

SERVES 4.

Grits are a part of many a meal down south. My grandson Prescott especially loves these cheese grits when I make it at dinner, or for his favorite meal, "breakfast for supper."

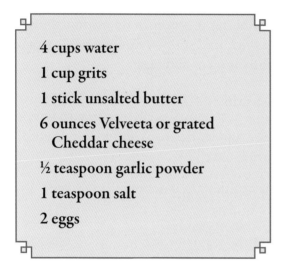

4 cups water

1 cup grits

1 stick unsalted butter

6 ounces Velveeta or grated
   Cheddar cheese

½ teaspoon garlic powder

1 teaspoon salt

2 eggs

1) Bring water to a boil in large saucepan. Add grits, and cook, stirring, until grits are done. Add butter, cheese, garlic powder, and salt, and stir until well mixed and cheese is melted.

2) Beat eggs in bowl. Slowly add 1 cup hot grits, stirring to warm eggs, then mix well.

3) Add egg mixture to remaining grits in saucepan, and blend thoroughly.

4) Pour grits into buttered 9x9-inch pan, and bake in preheated 350° oven 30 minutes.

5) Recipe doubles well. Baked grits will hold warm for an hour or more, tightly wrapped in aluminum foil. Serve warm.

TIDBIT: We've served cheese grits at late-night prom and graduation breakfasts, with Sausage Breakfast Casserole (page 50) for company breakfasts, and with sliced ham for Sunday lunch. And always when I serve my Shrimp and Grits (page 134), or New Orleans Beef Grillades (page 103)!

BAYOU RICE PILAF

SERVE 3–4.

What a lovely, colorful bed for grilled meats, or an entrée with a luscious sauce. Enjoy as a flavorful side dish anytime.

2 tablespoons unsalted butter

1 cup white rice

3 green onions, thinly sliced

2 cups chicken broth

½ teaspoon salt

½ cup sliced almonds (optional)

1) Melt butter in saucepan on medium heat. Add rice, and stir 3–4 minutes while rice lightly browns and toasts.

2) Mix in onions, broth, and salt. Bring to a boil, and immediately turn heat to low; cover, and let rice cook about 15 minutes, stirring once.

3) Stir in almonds, if desired, and serve.

TIDBIT: We serve this pilaf often with special dishes like Chicken Kiev (page 122) or Chicken Breast à la Orange (page 113), and I make it regularly at home. I usually double the recipe, and turn any "extra" rice into a salad with shredded fresh vegetables and a little vinaigrette dressing.

96

BEEF & PORK

Elizabethan Steak

STEAK AND MUSHROOM PIE

SERVES 4.

Meat pies of all types are a tradition in pubs and homes across the British Isles. I hope you will enjoy this simple flavorful version that our family loves.

1 cup flour

½ teaspoon salt

½ teaspoon coarsely ground
  black pepper

1½ pounds round steak, cut into
  thin strips about 2 inches long

½ stick or more butter, divided

1 onion, chopped

4 ounces fresh mushrooms,
  sliced

1 cup beef broth

½ cup red wine

1 sheet pie pastry

1 tablespoon milk

1) Combine flour, salt, and black pepper. Dip meat pieces into seasoned flour, shake off excess, and set aside until all are seasoned.

2) In large skillet over medium heat, melt 2 tablespoons butter; add half the meat, and lightly brown on both sides. Transfer to bowl. Add more butter, if needed, and cook remaining meat. Add meat to bowl.

3) Put remaining 2 tablespoons butter in same skillet, reduce heat to low, add onion and mushrooms, and toss in hot butter. Add broth, stirring and scraping to get all juices.

4) Return meat to skillet, add wine, and cook 5 minutes, stirring often. Transfer to a 9x9-inch buttered baking dish or deep-dish pie plate.

5) Center pastry sheet over dish. Press a half inch down into pie plate, sealing meat. Press overlapping pastry onto top edge to make a nice crimped rim.

6) Brush pastry, including edges, with a little milk. Make a loose tent of aluminum foil over pastry to prevent over browning. Bake in preheated 400° oven about 45 minutes.

ELIZABETHAN STEAK

SERVES 4.

This dinner party steak can be prepared hours before cooking. The cheeses melting inside the steak make the juices absolutely scrumptious! This was really enjoyed at wedding rehearsal parties when The Crown was in the cotton fields.

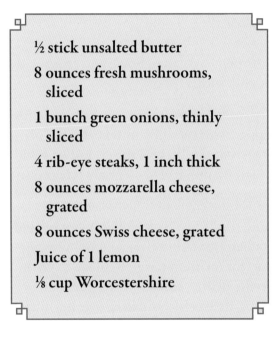

½ stick unsalted butter

8 ounces fresh mushrooms, sliced

1 bunch green onions, thinly sliced

4 rib-eye steaks, 1 inch thick

8 ounces mozzarella cheese, grated

8 ounces Swiss cheese, grated

Juice of 1 lemon

⅛ cup Worcestershire

TIP: To make a pocket, cut the side 1–2 inches wide, then slide knife around inside steak to make a nice pocket for the stuffing. Be careful to keep knife from cutting into top or bottom of steak.

1) Melt butter in skillet, add mushrooms and onions, and sauté on medium heat, until onions are just cooked, not browned. Set aside in a large bowl to cool.

2) Cut a pocket into side of each steak. Set aside.

3) Add cheeses to cooled mushroom mixture; stir to thoroughly combine stuffing.

4) Using a spoon, carefully insert a generous portion of stuffing into each steak pocket, filling it completely; then seal with a toothpick. Reserve any remaining stuffing. (At this point, steaks can be held refrigerated for several hours.)

5) Mix lemon and Worcestershire, and rub onto both sides of steaks. Broil 3–4 minutes per side (for medium rare).

6) Place extra stuffing on top of steaks. Leave in oven for a minute for cheeses to melt, and serve hot with buttered new potatoes or baked potatoes.

Steak Madagascar

SERVES 4.

We loved a little French restaurant outside Cambridge, England, called the DeLa Poste, and this steak was their specialty. We kept trying to re-create it at home, using a recipe in Julia Child's Art of French Cooking, but couldn't quite get it right. A friend who ate there with us suggested a dab of tomato paste, and that was the secret! Now it is Tony's specialty to cook for us on special occasions! Enjoy every drop of sauce with crusty bread.

2 tablespoons green peppercorns

4 beef fillet steaks, 1 inch thick

2 tablespoons oil

7 tablespoons butter, softened, divided

Pinch of salt

2 tablespoons minced green onions

½ cup beef broth

1 tablespoon tomato paste

⅓ cup brandy

1) Place peppercorns in bowl, and crush roughly with a spoon.

2) Dry steaks on paper towels. Rub and press peppercorns carefully into both sides of steaks, cover with wax paper, and let stand at least 30 minutes (2–3 hours is better so flavor penetrates meat).

3) Sauté steaks in a large skillet in hot oil and 2 tablespoons butter for 3–4 minutes per side (for medium rare.) Remove to warm serving platter, season with a pinch of salt on each steak, and keep warm while finishing sauce.

4) Pour drippings out of skillet; add 1 tablespoon butter and onions, and cook 1 minute, stirring. Add broth and tomato paste, and boil down rapidly over high heat, scraping up juices. Add brandy, and boil rapidly 1 minute to evaporate alcohol.

5) Remove from heat, then swirl in remaining 4 tablespoons butter, a little a time. Pour sauce over steaks, and serve. Serve any extra sauce in a small bowl on the table.

Steak Madagascar

New Orleans Beef Grillades

SERVES 12.

A scrumptious Louisiana dish with strips of beef simmered with bell peppers, onions, celery, and tomatoes in a red wine sauce that you can prepare ahead.

4 pounds lean beef (round steak or chuck roast)

½–1 cup oil, divided

½ cup all-purpose flour

2 medium onions, chopped (about 2 cups)

1 bunch green onions, sliced

3 stalks celery, finely chopped

2 green bell peppers, chopped (about 2 cups)

2 cloves garlic, minced

1 (8-ounce) can tomato sauce

1 teaspoon ground thyme

1 cup dry red wine

1–2 cups water, divided

2 teaspoons salt

1 teaspoon coarsely ground black pepper

2 tablespoons chopped parsley

1 teaspoon Tabasco

2 tablespoons Worcestershire

4 bay leaves

1) Cut meat into thin strips (about the size of your little finger). Dry meat on paper towels before browning.

2) In heavy Dutch oven, add enough oil to barely cover bottom of pan; heat on medium. Lightly brown meat a little at a time, so it is not crowded. As it browns, remove to a bowl, and continue cooking meat, adding more oil, if needed.

3) Add ½ cup oil to Dutch oven, sprinkle with flour, and stir constantly until flour is browned, and a rich roux forms. Immediately add onions, celery, bell peppers, and garlic, and stir until wilted.

4) Add tomato sauce, thyme, wine, and 1 cup water, stirring vigorously to make a smooth sauce.

5) Return meat to Dutch oven, gently folding into sauce. Add just enough additional water to cover meat, and stir until smooth.

6) Stir in salt, black pepper, parsley, Tabasco, Worcestershire, and bay leaves. Reduce heat to low, and simmer about 2 hours.

7) Serve immediately over rice or grits. Can be refrigerated 2–3 days, and heated just before serving. This dish freezes perfectly.

Mama's Sunday Beef Roast

SERVES 4–6.

It's called Sunday roast, because Mama put it on to cook before Sunday school so lunch was ready when we got home from church. The gravy is delicious, and the meat melts in your mouth. Mama always served the roast with mashed potatoes or rice, a green vegetable, and a salad of some sort. It might have been sliced tomatoes and onions, or pears on a bed of lettuce with a dab of mayonnaise in the center sprinkled with cheese. Mama wanted everything she cooked to be pretty and delicious.

1 (3- to 4-pound) beef roast

1 envelope Lipton Onion Soup mix

1 (10-ounce) can cream of mushroom soup

Pinch of salt

Pinch of black pepper

1) Line a pan just a little larger than the roast with enough foil to completely cover roast. Sprinkle onion soup mix over roast, then spread mushroom soup on top. Sprinkle with salt and black pepper.

2) Close foil tightly, and bake at 400° for 2½–3 hours. Serve hot.

WANDA'S WINNING SPANISH CASSEROLE

SERVES 6–8.

Mama made this casserole for as long as I can remember. It's easy, it tastes fresh, and it's a family tradition. When Wanda was in high school, she entered it in a student cooking contest and won! Later, her kids loved it so much, they enjoyed it once a week when she was teaching school. It's definitely a winner with our whole family, and Wanda is a winner to me!

1 large onion, chopped

1 large green bell pepper, chopped

2 tablespoons oil

1 pound ground beef

1 (15-ounce) can whole-kernel corn

1 (10-ounce) can tomato soup

2 (13-ounce) cans sliced mushrooms

1 small package egg noodles

1 cup grated Cheddar cheese

1) In large saucepan, cook onion and bell pepper in oil until tender.

2) Add ground beef, and brown, stirring constantly. Add corn, soup, and mushrooms, and stir well. Set aside.

3) Cook noodles in boiling water 5 minutes, drain, and stir noodles into meat mixture. Place in lightly buttered 9x13-inch baking dish. Sprinkle with cheese.

4) Bake in preheated 350° oven about 30 minutes. Casserole can be assembled the day before baking, and refrigerated.

Mama's Meatloaf in Crust

SERVES 6.

This recipe is my combination of Mama's, Jennifer's, and Julia Child's. My daughter Jennifer loved the fancy terrines she enjoyed in France that were served "en croute," which simply means baked in a crust. Good without the crust, too. But do try it.

2 tablespoons unsalted butter

1 onion, finely chopped

1 green bell pepper, finely chopped

2 pounds lean ground beef or turkey

2 eggs, beaten

1½ teaspoons salt

1 teaspoon coarsely ground black pepper

½ teaspoon ground thyme

¼ teaspoon allspice

1 teaspoon garlic powder

½ cup oatmeal

½ cup Jezebel Sauce (page 211), Tangy Tomato Dressing (page 75), or ketchup

1 (2-count) package refrigerated pie crust (optional)

Milk to glaze pastry

1) In skillet on medium heat, melt butter; add onion and bell pepper, and sauté until just tender. Transfer to large bowl.

2) Add ground meat, eggs, salt, black pepper, thyme, allspice, garlic powder, oatmeal, and Jezebel Sauce. Mix well. Set aside.

3) Place 1 prepared pie crust into lightly greased large loaf pan, letting edges drape over all sides. Spoon meat mixture into crust in pan, patting firmly and evenly. Place second crust on top, pinching edges of crusts together to seal.

4) Use trimmed crust to cut a pattern to lay on top crust, if you choose. Brush crust lightly with milk to glaze. Bake in preheated 350° oven about 1 hour.

5) To serve, remove from pan, and slice. Serve warm or cold.

SWEDISH MEATBALLS

SERVES 4–6.

We've enjoyed these meatballs for years, since we lived in England, as appetizers for small dinner parties, in chafing dishes at cocktail parties, and served them for supper over rice or noodles to my happy family.

3 tablespoons butter, divided

¼ cup finely minced onion

1½ pounds combination lean ground beef and pork

1 slice French bread, 1 inch thick, covered with milk or water

2 eggs, beaten

3 tablespoons chopped parsley

1¼ teaspoons salt

¼ teaspoon paprika

1 teaspoon grated lemon rind, divided

1 teaspoon fresh lemon juice

1 teaspoon Worcestershire

2 cups beef broth

1 tablespoon all-purpose flour

Dash of sherry

1) In small pan, melt 1 tablespoon butter, and sauté onion until golden.

2) Place meat in large bowl; add onion. Squeeze liquid from bread, and add bread to meat, mixing all thoroughly.

3) Add eggs, parsley, salt, paprika, ½ teaspoon lemon rind, lemon juice, and Worcestershire. Mix well. (Can be made a day before cooking, and refrigerated.)

4) Lightly shape into 1-inch balls with your hands. Set aside on cookie sheet.

5) Melt remaining 2 tablespoons butter in large skillet, and brown meatballs, without crowding. Transfer to Dutch oven as they brown.

6) Pour broth over meatballs, cover, and simmer 15 minutes. Pour broth into bowl, leaving meatballs in pan.

7) Heat 2 tablespoons drippings in browning skillet on medium heat; add flour, stirring until smooth and very lightly brown. Slowly add reserved broth, stirring to make a smooth gravy. Add sherry and remaining lemon rind. Pour gravy over meatballs.

THE CROWN'S
STUFFED PORK CHOPS

SERVES 4–6.

Pork chops have been the entrée at many special events at The Crown. So easy to prepare for a crowd, and then cook at the last minute before serving.

½ pound smoked sausage or Andouille

½ cup finely chopped green onions

1 apple, unpeeled, finely chopped

1 cup dry bread crumbs

½ teaspoon salt

½ teaspoon black pepper

4–6 pork chops, 1½ inches thick

½ teaspoon The Crown's Sassy Seasoning (page 218) or seasoned salt

1) Chop sausage into very small pieces. Brown sausage lightly in large skillet.

2) Add onions and apple, stirring for 2 minutes.

3) Stir in bread crumbs, salt, and black pepper, and combine well.

4) Cut a deep slit in the side of each pork chop, making a pocket. Use knife to make opening larger inside with a small opening on the side.

5) Fill each pork chop with stuffing, forcing it in so it bulges. Seal opening with toothpick. (At this point, pork chops will hold in refrigerator several hours.)

6) Lightly sprinkle both sides of chops with Sassy Seasoning. Cook pork chops under the broiler until done, about 5 minutes on each side. Serve hot.

TIP: Pork chops can be grilled.

ROAST PORK LOIN WITH APPLES AND APRICOTS

SERVES 6–8.

So simple to prepare, and such wonderful fresh flavor in the stuffing.

1 pound ground mild sausage

1 cup finely chopped celery

1 cup finely chopped onion

2 cups finely chopped apples (with peels)

1 cup dried apricots, chopped

⅔ cup dry bread crumbs

2 teaspoons salt

2 teaspoons ground thyme

½ teaspoon black pepper

1 (4- to 5-pound) pork loin

½ teaspoon The Crown's Sassy Seasoning (page 218) or seasoned salt

1 cup water

1) Cook sausage in large skillet until browned. Add celery and onion, and cook until just tender. Drain excess fat.

2) Add apples, apricots, bread crumbs, salt, thyme, and black pepper, and cook, stirring, 1 minute. Take off heat, and mix well. Set aside to cool. (At this point, stuffing can be refrigerated for several hours or overnight.)

3) Rub pork with Sassy Seasoning. Cut pork loin lengthwise, along the top of loin, leaving a half inch at each end, with the cut 2–3 inches deep. Fill cavity with stuffing. Close opening with skewers, toothpicks, or cooking twine. (At this point, pork can be covered tightly and refrigerated for several hours, or overnight, before cooking.)

4) When ready to cook, place pork loin in a covered roasting pan, and add 1 cup water. Bake in 325° oven about 3 hours. Slice, and serve hot or cold.

TIDBIT: I always prepare this early in the day on Christmas Eve, so I have time to get ready for our family party after church. Then, on Christmas morning, it just goes into the oven with no stress!

BEEF & PORK

Roast Pork Loin with Apples and Apricots

APRICOT-MUSTARD CRUSTED PORK CHOPS

SERVES 4.

Fruit and spices combine to make a flavorful simple supper to cook on top of the stove in the summer, or in the oven in the winter. Soooo good!

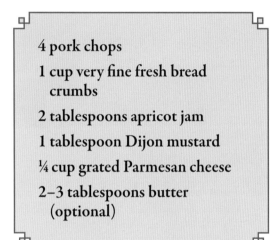

4 pork chops

1 cup very fine fresh bread crumbs

2 tablespoons apricot jam

1 tablespoon Dijon mustard

¼ cup grated Parmesan cheese

2–3 tablespoons butter (optional)

1) Wash pork chops and pat dry. Set aside.

2) Place bread crumbs in pie pan or flat dish.

3) In a small bowl, thoroughly combine jam, mustard, and cheese. Spread jam mixture on both sides of pork chops. Coat each with bread crumbs. Place in lightly buttered baking dish. (At this point, pork chops can be refrigerated several hours.)

4) In the winter, when ready to serve, place baking dish in preheated 350° oven 25–30 minutes, or until done. In the summer, melt butter in large skillet on medium heat, add pork chops, and sauté 4 minutes on each side, turning carefully, adding butter, if needed.

TIDBIT: Preparing food ahead of time and finishing it at the last minute is the way I really love to cook and entertain. I took to heart Julia Child's suggestions on how to prepare elements of the recipe ahead, with words like "if not serving immediately, refrigerate and reheat slowly." Prepare cut vegetables, measure out spices, set out utensils, and have the butter to sauté steaks or zucchini already in pan. All these small preparations, like the cooks on TV always do, let you enjoy your guests, and still cook for them at the last minute without hassle.

Chicken

The Crown's Chicken Thermidor

ACCIDENTAL ARTICHOKE CHICKEN

SERVES 6–8.

Artichoke chicken, incredibly tender meat in a creamy rich sauce, is now a favorite at The Crown, but it was created by accident, when I tried baking chicken smothered in Artichoke Dip (page 16). The dip was left over after a big party, and I am always trying to create new dishes. This experiment was a great success. I will always love "playing with food."

1 (14-ounce) can artichokes, well drained

2 (8-ounce) packages cream cheese, softened

¼ cup mayonnaise, or a bit more for softer texture

½ teaspoon The Crown's Sassy Seasoning (page 218) or seasoned salt

¼ teaspoon garlic powder

6–8 boneless chicken breasts

1) Place artichokes on cutting board, and cut into small pieces. Place artichokes, cream cheese, mayonnaise, Sassy Seasoning, and garlic powder in mixing bowl, and mix until well blended. (Sauce can be made several days ahead and refrigerated until ready to bake chicken.)

2) Place chicken in buttered 9x13-inch baking dish. Spoon all sauce over chicken. Cover tightly with aluminum foil, and bake in preheated 350° oven for 45 minutes.

3) Serve chicken over rice covered with all the sauce.

TIDBIT: When my children Jennifer and Kevin were growing up, they really didn't have an absolute favorite food. They told me after they were grown, they couldn't have a favorite, because I was always cooking something new and different...and they enjoyed everything.

CHICKEN BREAST À LA ORANGE

SERVES 4.

One of my friends calls this "Burnt Chicken," because I once served it very deeply browned. Sometimes I do get distracted, but it wasn't really burned, it was "caramelized" and totally delicious. The sauce on the chicken is almost candied under the broiler while it's layered several times. Its rich deep flavor makes this dish scrumptious.

4 chicken breasts, on bone

1 stick unsalted butter

1 large onion, chopped

½ cup chicken broth

1 cup frozen orange juice concentrate

1 cup currant or grape jelly

½ teaspoon crushed tarragon leaves

½ teaspoon salt

½ cup water

1 tablespoon cornstarch

Zest of 1 orange

1) Dry chicken well. In large skillet on medium heat, melt butter, and brown chicken on both sides. Transfer to baking dish that can be broiled, and set aside.

2) In same skillet, cook onion slowly, until transparent, stirring and scraping skillet. Add broth, orange juice, and jelly. Continue cooking, stirring constantly, while jelly melts. Stir in tarragon and salt.

3) Slowly add ½ cup water to cornstarch; whisk to dissolve. Drizzle into sauce, and stir vigorously to combine. Cook until sauce begins to thicken. Remove from heat. Stir in orange zest.

4) Pour sauce over chicken, cover, and bake in preheated 350° oven about 40 minutes.

5) Uncover chicken, stir sauce, and spoon over chicken; place under broiler. Keep oven door open, so you can see sauce bubbling. Spoon sauce over chicken several times, until it begins to brown. Cover, and keep warm.

6) Serve over rice pilaf, or plain rice, with sauce spooned over chicken.

THE CROWN'S CHICKEN ALLISON

SERVES 6.

Everyone's favorite—chicken breast, smothered in a rich Parmesan cheese sauce, broiled until well browned and toasted with all the juices, then served over rice. So simple to make...just be sure to brown that sauce deeply.

6 boneless chicken breasts

½ teaspoon black pepper

½ teaspoon salt

1 lemon, sliced

ALLISON BUTTER:

1 cup grated Parmesan cheese

½ cup butter (no substitutes)

6 tablespoons mayonnaise

½ teaspoon Worcestershire

½ teaspoon Tabasco

6 green onions, finely diced

1) Poach chicken breasts in lightly simmering water (enough to cover chicken) with black pepper, salt, and lemon, until cooked through. Gently lift chicken from water, and set aside to drain.

2) For Allison Butter, combine Parmesan, butter, mayonnaise, Worcestershire, and Tabasco in a mixing bowl, and blend thoroughly.

3) Add green onions, and stir with a spoon. Allison Butter can be used immediately, or made 2 weeks ahead and kept refrigerated. Just let mixture soften a little before using.

4) When you are ready to serve, place chicken on a large pan or cookie sheet that can be used under a broiler. Cover each chicken breast with 2 tablespoons (or more) of Allison Butter. Broil until butter mixture has browned deeply...not lightly browned. The nutty flavor of butter comes from the deep browning. Serve over rice with pan juices poured over chicken.

TIDBIT: This is the chicken variation of our original Catfish Allison, and is one of the favorite dishes at The Crown, both for individual guests, and for international tour groups who join us for lunch. Everyone loves the chicken with juicy rice, so the more Allison Butter you use, the happier your guests will be. For a buffet, layer rice in serving dish, then top with chicken and all juices. So easy, and so delicious!

The Crown's Chicken Allison

CHICKEN BREASTS WITH LEMON CREAM SAUCE

SERVES 4.

This has a lovely fresh citrus flavor, and the broiled sauce is scrumptious! Guests have enjoyed this at luncheons since we were in the cotton fields, and we love to serve it at home. The sauce is amazing!

4 chicken breasts, bone in, skin removed

1 stick butter

1 lemon, zested then sliced

1 orange, zested then sliced

⅛ teaspoon black pepper

½ teaspoon salt

1¼ cups evaporated milk or half-and-half

½ cup grated Cheddar cheese

1) Pat chicken breasts dry with paper towels. Place butter in large skillet on medium heat. When butter is hot and bubbling, put chicken into skillet, meaty side down, until browned. Turn breast over, cover skillet, and cook slowly until chicken is almost done.

2) Remove chicken from skillet; add lemon and orange zest, black pepper, and salt. Slowly add milk, stirring constantly to make the sauce smooth.

3) Return chicken to pan, turning to cover with sauce. Remove from heat.

4) Place chicken into broiler-safe baking pan. Spoon sauce over chicken, and sprinkle with cheese. Broil until cheese is melted, then spoon on more sauce, and broil again. Repeat this process until sauce is browned.

5) Garnish plates with orange and lemon slices. Serve chicken over rice; cover with all the sauce from broiling pan.

Cotton fields abound in the Delta. A cotton boll, as seen here, is often used as decoration.

CARD PARTY CHICKEN

A favorite of our bridge players when The Crown was in the cotton fields, we usually served this on a rice pilaf with marinated asparagus and a congealed fruit salad because it would hold if the card game went on longer than expected. And because it's so delicious!

1 (8-ounce) package dried beef or pastrami

8 boneless chicken breasts, pounded flat

1 cup sour cream

1 (10-ounce) can cream of mushroom soup

4 green onions, finely diced

1 teaspoon Worcestershire

½ teaspoon The Crown's Sassy Seasoning (page 218) or seasoned salt

1 teaspoon parsley flakes

1 teaspoon soy sauce

10 drops Tabasco sauce

1) Slice dried beef into small pieces, and sprinkle half evenly into a buttered 9x13-inch baking dish.

2) Put a teaspoon of remaining dried beef in center of each chicken breast, fold breast over, and place in baking dish.

3) In a bowl, mix sour cream, soup, onions, Worcestershire, Sassy Seasoning, parsley, soy sauce, and Tabasco, and combine thoroughly. Cover chicken breasts with mixture.

4) Cover tightly, and bake in preheated 300° oven 2 hours.

5) Serve over rice with all the gravy. Chicken will hold for an hour before serving, if tightly covered and kept warm.

THE CROWN'S CHICKEN THERMIDOR

SERVES 6–8.

The creamy rich sauce is simply heavenly. I like to serve it over rice with a big scoop of My Favorite Green Bean Salad (page 72). The tart salad is perfect with the rich sauce. This is frequently my choice for a memorable main dish.

CHICKEN

1 stick unsalted butter

6–8 chicken breasts, cut in 1-inch cubes

¼ cup finely chopped yellow onion

1 cup thinly sliced fresh mushrooms

5 tablespoons all-purpose flour

1½ cups milk

1 cup heavy cream

1 teaspoon dry mustard

1 teaspoon celery salt

1½ teaspoons salt

¼ teaspoon cayenne pepper

3 egg yolks, beaten (save the whites for Pavlova, page 198)

1 cup grated Swiss cheese

4 tablespoons dry white wine

Juice of 1 lemon

1) Melt butter in large pot on medium heat. Stir in half the chicken, cooking until chicken turns white; transfer to a bowl. Cook remaining chicken; set aside.

2) To same pan, add onion and mushrooms, cooking and stirring 2 minutes. Add flour, and stir until smooth and bubbly. Slowly add milk, then cream, stirring constantly until thickened and smooth. Stir in mustard, celery salt, salt, and cayenne pepper, mixing together well.

3) Gradually add 2 tablespoons mixture to egg yolks, stirring rapidly, then stir warmed yolks slowly into sauce. Add cheese, wine, and lemon juice, stirring until smooth.

4) Turn heat to low. Return chicken with accumulated juices to pan, stirring gently to cover chicken completely. Cook slowly, stirring gently, until chicken is fully cooked, 10–12 minutes.

5) Serve immediately over rice, or in baked, individual pastry shells.

LOUISIANA CHICKEN AND SAUSAGE

SERVES 6–8.

We love this meal in the winter, and of course during Mardi Gras! At The Crown, we cut the chicken into small pieces to sauté with the sausage, then serve it over rice in individual dishes with all the delicious juices.

1 pound smoked sausage, cut into thin slices

1 onion, diced

1 green bell pepper, diced

6–8 chicken thighs, bone in with skin removed (or boneless)

1 (26-ounce) can diced tomatoes

¾ cup hot water

1 teaspoon chicken broth powder or granules

1 teaspoon salt

1 teaspoon black pepper

Dash of Tabasco (optional)

1) Place sausage in large saucepan or Dutch oven over medium heat, and cook 5 minutes.

2) Drain excess grease from pan, and add onion, bell pepper, and chicken, stirring constantly for a few minutes so chicken does not stick to pan.

3) Add tomatoes, water, and chicken broth. Stir well, cover, and cook slowly for about 30 minutes, until chicken is cooked. Taste and adjust seasonings.

4) Set aside, refrigerated, until ready to heat. Serve over rice. Flavors blend well when held overnight or up to 2 days.

Hambone (Alex Brown) has worked at the Crown for 18 years, and is a much loved symbol of friendship in downtown Indianola. Louisiana Chicken and Sausage is always what he wants for lunch!

POPPY SEED CHICKEN

SERVES 6.

The popularity of Poppy Seed Chicken around Indianola for many, many years makes this a classic Delta dish!

6 boneless or bone-in chicken breasts

1 (10-ounce) can cream of chicken soup

1 (16-ounce) carton sour cream

1 teaspoon salt

1 teaspoon coarsely ground black pepper

1½ tablespoons poppy seeds

1 roll Ritz Crackers, crushed

1 stick unsalted butter, melted

1) Boil chicken in water to cover. Cool. Debone chicken, and cut into small pieces. Place chicken in large bowl, add soup, sour cream, salt, black pepper, and poppy seeds; mix well.

2) Place mixture in lightly buttered 11x7-inch baking dish, or larger. Mix crushed crackers with butter, and sprinkle evenly over top.

3) Bake in preheated 400° oven about 45 minutes. Serve hot.

TIP: The prepared casserole can be made the day before using, and kept refrigerated. Poppy Seed Chicken freezes perfectly. Simply thaw overnight in the refrigerator, and bake as directed. Tastes wonderful served over rice! I always keep a dish in the freezer, ready to enjoy or take to a friend.

Poppy Seed Chicken

121

CHICKEN KIEV

SERVES 8.

An elegant rolled chicken breast sitting on a rice pilaf ready to be sliced, so the juicy butter hidden inside can pour from the chicken onto the rice. Truly a meal fit for a king.

1 stick plus 2 tablespoons unsalted butter, softened, divided

¼ cup chopped chives or green onions

½ teaspoon black pepper

1½ teaspoons grated lemon peel

2 tablespoons fresh lemon juice

8 boneless chicken breasts

1 cup flour

2 eggs, beaten

2 cups dry bread crumbs or Crispy Crumbles (page 80)

2 tablespoons oil, for browning

1) In mixing bowl, combine 1 stick butter, chives, black pepper, lemon peel, and juice; mix well. Make tablespoon-size balls of this flavored butter mixture. Refrigerate until needed.

2) Place chicken breasts skin side down on large sheet of plastic wrap, and cover with more wrap. Flatten breasts by pounding gently with rolling pin, being careful not to break through the skin.

3) Place 1 ball of butter mixture in middle of each breast. Pull both sides of breast gently to cover the ball, then roll breast tightly from one end to completely cover butter. Secure with toothpick.

4) Place flour, eggs, and bread crumbs in 3 separate bowls. Roll chicken in flour, then eggs, then bread crumbs.

5) In a skillet, heat remaining 2 tablespoons butter and 2 tablespoons oil on medium. Brown breaded Chicken Kiev, a few at a time, very lightly, turning gently to brown all sides.

6) When ready to serve, bake Kiev in preheated 350° oven about 25 minutes. Serve on a bed of rice, so juices escape into the rice when the Chicken Kiev is cut.

SUFFOLK CHICKEN CURRY

SERVES 4.

This English-style pub curry is not meant to be hot and spicy, but simply meant to tempt your taste buds with exotic, fresh flavor, and beautiful color for a delicious meal.

1 cup all-purpose flour

1 teaspoon salt

¼ teaspoon black pepper

1 teaspoon cumin

4 chicken breasts, bone in

½ stick unsalted butter

1 apple, peeled, chopped finely

1 onion, chopped

1 clove garlic, minced

1 tablespoon curry powder

½ teaspoon ground thyme

1 (26-ounce) can petite diced tomatoes

1) Combine flour, salt, black pepper, and cumin, and mix well.

2) Dip chicken in seasoned flour, coating well.

3) In a large skillet, melt butter, and brown chicken on both sides. Drain, then transfer chicken to a baking dish.

4) To same skillet, add apple, onion, garlic, curry, and thyme, and simmer gently until onions are golden, stirring well.

5) Add tomatoes, and simmer 10 minutes more, stirring to mix all ingredients.

6) Pour sauce over chicken, and bake uncovered in preheated 350° oven 45 minutes.

7) Serve over rice with lots of sauce and fruit chutney, if desired. (Curry will hold refrigerated overnight; warm slowly to serve.)

TIDBIT: English pubs and hotels in the 60's offered curry on the menu, and we loved the subtle flavors of their English version of Indian food! Our favorite was The Bell Hotel in Clare, where we could sit by the fireplace in the lounge (kids weren't welcomed in dining rooms) with Jennifer and Kevin playing on the floor and all of us enjoying their delightful curry served with fried papadams.

CHICKEN AND MUSHROOM CRÊPES

SERVES 8–10.

Two of these crêpes are very filling, so for a ladies luncheon, I suggest a fresh fruit salad on a bed of mixed greens with a little Poppy Seed Dressing (page 78). Make your own crêpes (page 43) or purchase packaged crêpes.

CREAM SAUCE:

½ stick unsalted butter

4 tablespoons all-purpose flour

2 cups milk

2 tablespoons dry white wine

1 teaspoon dry mustard

¼ teaspoon garlic powder

½ teaspoon salt

FILLING:

5 cups cubed cooked chicken

1 (8-ounce) can sliced mushrooms, drained

5 green onions, minced

½ teaspoon ground cumin

1 teaspoon salt

½ teaspoon black pepper

TO FINISH:

8–10 crêpes

1–2 cups grated Swiss cheese

Paprika to garnish

1) For Cream Sauce, melt butter in saucepan over medium heat; add flour and cook, stirring to make a roux. Slowly add milk, ½ cup at a time, and stir until smooth. Stir in wine, mustard, garlic, and salt until thickened. Set Cream Sauce aside.

2) For Filling, combine chicken, mushrooms, onions, cumin, salt, and black pepper in large bowl; mix well. Stir in 3 tablespoons prepared Cream Sauce.

3) To finish, place Filling down center of each crêpe, folding one end over, pulling slightly to tighten, then roll into a cylinder. (Can refrigerate or freeze in airtight container.) Place filled crêpes on lightly buttered baking sheets, in pairs.

4) Spoon 2 tablespoons Cream Sauce over each pair, taking care to cover ends of crêpes. Sprinkle with cheese. Refrigerate until ready to serve.

5) To serve, place crêpes under a hot broiler until hot and cheese is melted, about 5 minutes. Serve garnished with paprika.

AUNT LENORE'S HARVEST MOON CASSEROLE

SERVES 8.

Harvest moon is a treasure, because it can be made ahead to serve at big family gatherings, and uses only healthy, fresh ingredients. In the 60's, Wanda collected recipes from all our family and wrote them by hand in a notebook she still uses. Her notebook has recovered some of my recipes I thought I had lost. My sister, Wanda is our treasured food historian.

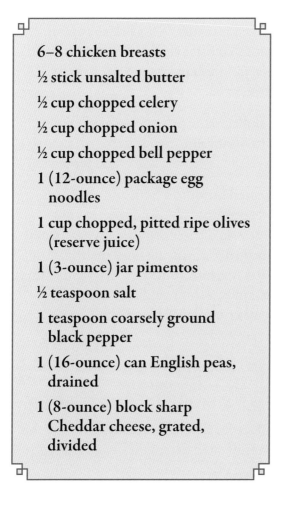

6–8 chicken breasts

½ stick unsalted butter

½ cup chopped celery

½ cup chopped onion

½ cup chopped bell pepper

1 (12-ounce) package egg noodles

1 cup chopped, pitted ripe olives (reserve juice)

1 (3-ounce) jar pimentos

½ teaspoon salt

1 teaspoon coarsely ground black pepper

1 (16-ounce) can English peas, drained

1 (8-ounce) block sharp Cheddar cheese, grated, divided

1) Put chicken in heavy pan, cover with water, bring to a boil, reduce heat to low, and cook gently until done, about 30 minutes. Take chicken off bone, and shred into small pieces; do not chop. Set aside, and reserve broth.

2) In large pot over medium heat, melt butter; add celery, onion, and bell pepper, and cook 2–3 minutes. Add 6 cups reserved broth. (If more is needed, use bouillon cubes with water for difference.) Bring to a boil, and add noodles. Cook until almost done. Add olives, pimentos, salt, and black pepper.

3) Add chicken and peas to pot, and mix gently. Pour half of chicken mixture into buttered 9x13-inch pan. Smooth, and sprinkle with half the cheese. Add remaining mixture, smooth, and sprinkle with remaining cheese. (Can be frozen; thaw completely before baking.)

4) Cover, and bake at 325° for 45 minutes. Uncover, and bake an additional 15 minutes. Serve immediately.

DELTA CHICKEN SPAGHETTI

SERVE 10–12.

Chicken spaghetti is a meal everyone in the Delta loves. In the old days, when Mama made chicken spaghetti, it was a little less spicy. She used plain tomatoes with a few red pepper flakes, so if you don't want the chiles, do it Mama's way.

2 pounds, boneless chicken thighs or breasts

½ teaspoon salt

½ teaspoon garlic powder

½ teaspoon coarsely ground black pepper

2 large green bell peppers, chopped

2 large onions, chopped

1 stick unsalted butter

1 (16-ounce) package vermicelli

2 pounds Velveeta cheese, cubed

2 (10-ounce) cans diced tomatoes with green chiles

2 tablespoons Worcestershire

1 (15-ounce) can English peas, drained

1 (13-ounce) can sliced mushrooms, drained

1) Place chicken, salt, garlic powder, and black pepper in large pan. Cover with water. Cook on medium heat until chicken is tender. Set aside to cool in broth. Transfer chicken to cutting board, and cut into bite-size pieces. Reserve broth.

2) In skillet, sauté bell peppers and onions in butter until soft. Set aside.

3) Into a very large pot, bring 6–8 cups reserved broth to a boil; add vermicelli, and cook until almost done. Do not overcook. Leave vermicelli in broth; add cubed cheese, stirring until melted. Add onion mixture, tomatoes, Worcestershire, peas, mushrooms, and chicken. Fold together until well blended.

4) Pour into lightly buttered 9x13-inch (or larger) baking dish or 2 or 3 smaller dishes.

5) Bake in preheated 350° oven 45 minutes.

TIP: Freezes well before baking, and can be held refrigerated overnight before baking. Having an extra pan in the freezer really comes in handy for when you are hungry but too tired to cook, or want to take a meal to a friend.

Delta Chicken Spaghetti

KING RANCH CHICKEN CASSEROLE

SERVES 6.

Moist and spicy, this chicken dish will be a favorite at your house, like it is at ours. Our Texas friend made it for us in 1969 when we were living in England, and our English friends loved it, too.

1 large onion, chopped

1 large green bell pepper, chopped

2 tablespoons oil

2 cups chopped cooked chicken

1 (10-ounce) can cream of chicken soup

1 (10-ounce) can cream of mushroom soup

1 (10-ounce) can diced tomatoes with green chiles

1 teaspoon chili powder

¼ teaspoon salt

½ teaspoon garlic powder

½ teaspoon coarsely ground black pepper

12 (6-inch) corn tortillas

2 cups grated Cheddar cheese, divided

1) In a large skillet, cook onion and bell pepper in oil over medium heat until tender, stirring well. Add chicken, both soups, tomatoes, chili powder, salt, garlic powder, and black pepper, and mix well.

2) Cut or rip tortillas into small pieces. Put one-third of tortillas in lightly buttered 9x13-inch baking pan. Top with one-third of chicken mixture and one-third of cheese. Repeat layers, ending with cheese.

3) Bake in preheated 350° oven 30–35 minutes, until bubbling.

TIP: Casserole can be made and refrigerated overnight before baking, and it will freeze well. Thaw frozen dish in refrigerator overnight before baking.

MAMA'S CHICKEN AND RICE

SERVES 6–8.

We had a hot meal every night growing up—sandwiches at lunch, but a big meal at night. Chicken and rice was an easy meal, and Mama made it often. She was a home-economics major, and loved the convenience of the 1940's and 1950's shortcuts for main dishes. She would work for hours on desserts and special foods, but loved to throw a casserole together. When Daddy would be off on a trip, we would have asparagus on toast or chicken à la king, and other foods that Daddy didn't like—but Mama loved. Tony and I still have a hot meal every night—it's tradition!

1 (10-ounce) can cream of mushroom soup

1 soup can water

¾ envelope Lipton's Onion Soup mix

½ teaspoon salt

1 teaspoon finely ground black pepper

6–8 pieces of chicken (thighs and breasts)

1 cup uncooked rice

1) In a medium bowl, mix soup, water, onion soup mix, salt, and black pepper, and stir well.

2) Place chicken in buttered 9x13-inch baking dish.

3) Pour half the soup mixture over chicken. Sprinkle rice over and around chicken. Pour remaining soup mixture into dish, and spread evenly.

4) Cover, and cook in preheated 350° oven 1 hour, then reduce heat to 300°, and cook another hour.

MISSISSIPPI CHICKEN AND DRESSING

SERVES 6–8.

In our family, chicken and dressing is the main attraction at Sunday lunch, not the side dish to a turkey at Thanksgiving. Now, we have a big pan of cornbread dressing with the turkey for sure, but it won't have all the chicken baked in the dressing—a little but not much. Momo would make chicken and dressing on Saturday, and refrigerate it to bake after church on Sunday. It was always a feast with butter beans, black-eyed peas, baked sweet potatoes, deviled eggs, pickled peaches, sliced tomatoes, pickles, rolls, and pies or peach cobbler for dessert. She never knew how many people would be there to eat, so lots of side dishes took care of a crowd. Every dish was passed around the table, and everyone had plenty. Sweet memories of family and wonderful meals together.

3 pounds chicken thighs

1 large onion, chopped

6 ribs celery, chopped

2 tablespoons unsalted butter

1 pan Mama's Buttermilk Cornbread (page 40), crumbled

2 (10-ounce) cans cream of chicken soup

1 teaspoon salt

1 teaspoon poultry seasoning

3–4 cups chicken broth

3 boiled eggs, chopped

1) Place chicken in large saucepan, cover with water, and cook until done.

2) When chicken is cooked, transfer to cutting board, reserving broth. When cool, debone chicken, and cut into pieces.

3) In saucepan, cook onion and celery in butter until tender. Transfer to large bowl. Add chicken, cornbread, soup, salt, poultry seasoning, and 3 cups reserved chicken broth. Mix well. Fold in chopped eggs. Add additional broth, if needed.

4) Lightly butter a 9x13-inch baking dish. Pour chicken mixture into dish, and bake in preheated 350° oven 35–40 minutes, until lightly browned. (Dish holds well refrigerated overnight before baking.)

SEAFOOD

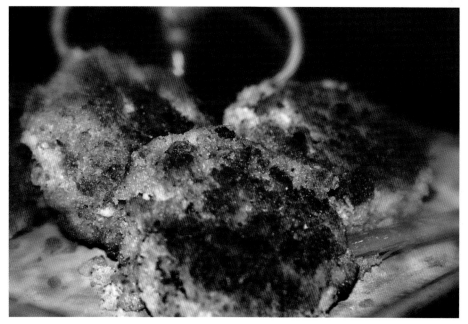

Creole Catfish Cakes with Peach Salsa

Catfish Allison

SERVES 6–8.

Claudia Ainsworth shared this recipe—named for her daughter—with us years ago, when we both entered a catfish cooking contest. Neither of us won, but Catfish Allison has become a favorite at The Crown because the sauce is so rich and good, you just have to capture every drop of it.

SEAFOOD

6–8 U.S. Farm-Raised Catfish fillets

½ teaspoon salt

½ teaspoon black pepper

1 lemon, sliced

ALLISON BUTTER:

1 cup grated Parmesan cheese

1 stick butter (no substitute), softened

6 tablespoons mayonnaise

½ teaspoon Worcestershire

½ teaspoon Tabasco

6 green onions, chopped very fine

TIP: Serve with Crisp Zucchini Sauté (page 86) or Black Butter Green Beans (page 86).

1) Poach catfish fillets in a large skillet in lightly simmering water (enough to cover fish) with salt, black pepper, and lemon slices 4–5 minutes. Gently lift fillets from water, and set aside to drain. (Fillets can be refrigerated overnight before serving.)

2) For Allison Butter, place cheese, butter, mayonnaise, Worcestershire, and Tabasco in a mixing bowl, and blend thoroughly. Gently stir in green onions by hand. (Can be made 2 weeks ahead and kept refrigerated. Soften a little before using.)

3) For individual servings, place fillets in au gratin dishes; cover with 2 tablespoons Allison Butter. Place dishes under hot broiler, and brown deeply for more flavor.

4) Otherwise, place fillets on lightly buttered cookie sheet with sides. Cover each with Butter; brown deeply under hot broiler. Carefully lift each fillet onto a bed of rice on each individual plate, and spoon juices over fillets.

*Catfish Allison
with The Crown's
Black Butter Green
Beans (page 86)*

BLACK BUTTER CATFISH

SERVES 6.

Black Butter Catfish was the first catfish entrée served at The Crown. We tasted the butter in France, years ago, served over fish. It is now an all-time favorite, especially for Tony!

SEAFOOD

3 cups water

1 lemon, thinly sliced

¼ teaspoon coarsely black pepper

¼ teaspoon salt

6 U.S. Farm-Raised Catfish fillets (or cod, tilapia, etc.)

6–8 tablespoons Black Butter (page 215)

2 tablespoons sliced almonds, toasted

2 lemons, quartered, to garnish

1) Place water, sliced lemon, black pepper, and salt in large skillet, and heat on medium until barely simmering. Add catfish, and simmer 6–8 minutes. Lift fish onto a plate to drain.

2) When ready to serve, place cooked fish in individual au gratin dishes (or a baking dish to hold them all in 1 layer). Spoon warm Black Butter on each fillet. Heat 15–20 minutes in preheated 350° oven until bubbly.

3) Sprinkle fish with almonds, and serve with a wedge of lemon.

FLORENTINE CATFISH

SERVES 6–8.

Delicious hot from the oven without broiling, but the flavor is enhanced with the browned cheese! The catfish industry was off to a strong start in the early 80's in the Delta, and I was determined to find great ways to serve catfish—other than fried. My guests at The Crown also wanted our local crop to flourish, and encouraged me to try new catfish dishes. It became a mission with us.

3 cups water

1 lemon, thinly sliced

6–8 U.S. Farm-Raised Catfish fillets, or other fish

1 (10-ounce) package frozen, chopped spinach

½ stick butter

1 clove garlic, minced

3 green onions, finely chopped

4 tablespoons flour

2 cups milk

3 teaspoons fresh lemon juice

1 cup grated Swiss cheese, divided

½ teaspoon dry mustard

½ teaspoon freshly ground black pepper

1 teaspoon salt

1) In large saucepan, bring water and lemon to slow simmer. Add catfish, and poach about 8 minutes; drain.

2) Thaw spinach, and drain. Squeeze moisture from spinach with towel.

3) Melt butter in heavy saucepan on medium heat. Add garlic and onions, and cook to soften. Add flour, and stir constantly. Do not brown. Slowly stir in milk until sauce is smooth and thickened. Add lemon juice, ½ cup cheese, mustard, black pepper, and salt, stirring to melt cheese.

4) Take off heat, add spinach, and combine thoroughly.

5) Place cooked catfish in lightly buttered 9x13-inch broiler-safe baking dish (or individual au gratin dishes). Cover fish with sauce and remaining ½ cup cheese.

6) Bake in preheated 350° oven about 15 minutes, until bubbly. Finish under oven broiler to lightly toast cheese. Serve immediately.

MISSISSIPPI DELTA FRIED CATFISH

SERVES 6–8.

We love our fried catfish in the South! Fry the whole fillet of fish, or make strips as I suggest here. Strips fry quicker and also make a great appetizer for parties. Wedding receptions across the Delta often include fried strips, because our men love their catfish!

8 U.S. Farm-Raised Catfish fillets

1 cup buttermilk

2 teaspoons The Crown's Sassy Seasoning (page 218) or seasoned salt

2 cups cornmeal

½ cup all-purpose flour

Oil for frying (peanut oil preferred)

1) Wash catfish, and pat dry. Cut fillets down the middle to make strips. Place fish in shallow pan, and pour buttermilk over. Rub milk onto fish, then turn fish over in pan to coat other side with buttermilk.

2) Sprinkle fish very lightly with Sassy Seasoning, then mix remaining Sassy Seasoning with cornmeal and flour in a large paper bag (or deep bowl).

3) Place fish, a few at a time, into cornmeal mixture, and shake the bag to cover fish completely. Set fish aside on cookie sheet, while breading remaining fish.

4) Heat oil to 375°, and fry fish a few at a time, until lightly browned. Do not crowd fish in oil. To keep fish warm after frying, place cooked fillets in a brown paper bag, and close tightly.

5) Serve immediately. For the perfect Delta fish fry, serve fish with Mama's Hushpuppies (page 41), french fries, coleslaw, ketchup, and lemon.

SEAFOOD

Mississippi Delta Fried Catfish with Mama's Marinated Coleslaw (page 74)

CREOLE CATFISH CAKES WITH PEACH SALSA

SERVES 4–6.

SEAFOOD

PEACH SALSA:

1 cup prepared salsa

1 cup peach preserves

CREOLE CATFISH CAKES:

6 U.S. Farm-Raised Catfish fillets (or cod, haddock, etc.)

1 lemon, thinly sliced

½ teaspoon salt

1 stick butter, divided

¾ cup flour

2 cups milk

½ teaspoon black pepper

½ teaspoon dry mustard

1½ cups finely chopped green bell pepper

½ cup finely chopped green onions

½ teaspoon Tabasco

2 cups fresh bread crumbs

2 tablespoons oil

1) Combine salsa with preserves; refrigerate.

2) Poach catfish in water to cover in skillet or pan, add lemon and salt, and bring to a slight simmer. Cook gently about 8 minutes; drain well. Flake catfish into large bowl.

3) Melt 6 tablespoons butter in heavy saucepan. Add flour, and stir constantly until roux bubbles. Slowly add milk, stirring until sauce is thick, 10–12 minutes. Add black pepper and mustard, and stir until smooth. Set aside.

4) Add warm sauce to catfish, then stir in bell pepper, onions, Tabasco, and ¾ cup bread crumbs; mix well. Refrigerate mixture until firm enough to handle, or overnight.

5) Form flat cakes from catfish mixture. Coat each with bread crumbs, turning gently and patting to coat lightly with crumbs. (At this point, cakes can be frozen, very tightly wrapped for a month.)

6) In a heavy skillet, heat oil and remaining 2 tablespoons butter, then sauté a few cakes at a time until browned.

7) Serve with Peach Salsa drizzled over top.

Catfish Royale

SERVES 6–8.

One of the joys of this dish is how easily it can be made early in the day, and finished at the last minute when you are ready to serve guests. Carolyn Ann Sledge and I served Catfish Royale to a large group of food editors from across the country who were touring the Mississippi Delta's catfish industry in 1983. Using classic French sauces on our southern catfish convinced these writers that U.S. Farm-Raised Catfish was as wonderful as any other firm white fish, and it did not "have to be fried" to be enjoyed.

6–8 U.S. Farm-Raised Catfish fillets (or tilapia, haddock, etc.)

1 bay leaf

1 lemon, sliced

Dash of salt and black pepper

2 tablespoons unsalted butter

2 tablespoons all-purpose flour

1 cup milk

2 tablespoons dry white wine

1 teaspoon dry mustard

¼ teaspoon garlic powder

½ teaspoon salt

1 cup Simple Hollandaise Sauce (page 214)

½ pound crabmeat and/or cooked, peeled shrimp

1) Place fish, bay leaf, lemon, salt, and black pepper in a large saucepan or skillet, cover with water, and simmer slowly 6–8 minutes. Remove, and drain fish.

2) In medium saucepan, melt butter; add flour, stirring constantly, allowing it to bubble for 1 minute or so. Do not brown. Slowly add milk, continuing to stir while sauce thickens. Add wine, mustard, garlic, and salt, stirring cream sauce until smooth.

3) Into pan of cream sauce, add Hollandaise Sauce and crabmeat or shrimp (or both), stirring gently to blend.

4) Place fish on lightly buttered baking dish, and cover with sauce.

5) When ready to serve, place fish in preheated 400° oven 8–10 minutes until sauce is lightly browned.

6) Serve on a bed of rice with roasted vegetables or buttered fresh asparagus.

SHRIMP STUFFED FISH FILLETS

SERVES 6–8.

In July 1984, Southern Living magazine included The Crown in an article about restaurants specializing in catfish. We developed this recipe for their visit and the article.

SEAFOOD

STUFFING:

1 small onion, minced

3 green onions, minced

4 ounces fresh mushrooms, sliced

3 tablespoons unsalted butter

½ cup soft bread crumbs

3 tablespoons chopped parsley

Juice of 1 lemon

½ pound shrimp, cooked, peeled

SAUCE:

½ stick unsalted butter

4 tablespoons flour

2⅔ cups milk

2 egg yolks

⅓ cup dry white wine

½ teaspoon dry mustard

⅛ teaspoon cayenne pepper

¼ teaspoon salt

FISH ROLLS:

6–8 U.S. Farm-Raised Catfish fillets (or tilapia, snapper, cod)

¾ cup grated Swiss cheese

1) Sauté onions and mushrooms in butter until tender. Add bread crumbs, parsley, lemon juice, and shrimp, mixing well. (Stuffing will hold refrigerated 24 hours.)

2) For Sauce, melt butter in heavy saucepan on low heat. Add flour, and cook 1 minute, stirring until smooth and bubbling. Slowly add milk, stirring as sauce thickens. Beat egg yolks, then stir a little Sauce into eggs to warm. Stir eggs slowly into Sauce. Stir in wine, mustard, cayenne, and salt. Sauce will hold refrigerated overnight.

3) Wash fish, and pat dry. Spread 2 tablespoons or more Stuffing across center of each fillet. Roll fillets, and secure with toothpick. Place seam side down in lightly buttered broiler-safe baking pan. Spoon a bit of Sauce over each roll. Bake at 350° for 25 minutes. (Fish Rolls can be refrigerated 24 hours and finished in a hot oven just before serving.)

4) When ready to serve, place fish rolls in individual baking dishes, or leave in baking pan. Spoon remaining Sauce over rolls. Sprinkle with cheese. Bake 15 minutes to reheat. Place under broiler to melt and brown cheese. Serve hot.

Shrimp Stuffed Fish Fillets (above, in baking dish before; and below, in individual dish after)

Sybil's Parmesan Catfish

SERVES 6–8.

Craig Claiborne, The New York Times food editor for many years, enjoyed this dish at my good friend Sybil Arant's home while visiting his hometown of Indianola in the 1980's. He wrote about the trip and her catfish dish in his column. In late 2014, a Mississippi Historical Marker was placed in front of his childhood home on Percy Street to honor this culinary pioneer.

1 tablespoon milk

1 egg, beaten

¾ cup finely grated Parmesan cheese

¼ cup all-purpose flour

¼ teaspoon salt

½ teaspoon black pepper

1 teaspoon paprika

6–8 U.S. Farm-Raised Catfish fillets (or other fish fillets)

¼ cup unsalted butter, melted

¼ cup sliced almonds, crushed

1) Combine milk and egg in a pie pan or bowl. Combine cheese, flour, salt, black pepper and paprika in another pie pan or flat dish.

2) Dip each fish fillet into milk mixture, then into cheese mixture, coating both sides. Place fish in 1 layer on a lightly buttered, flat baking pan. Do not crowd fish. (The fish may be held refrigerated at this point for several hours.)

3) When ready to serve, drizzle butter over fish, and top with almonds. Bake in preheated 325° oven about 40 minutes, until fish and almonds are crisp and golden.

SEAFOOD

BAKED EGGPLANT WITH SHRIMP

SERVES 6.

Craig Claiborne shared this recipe on one of his visits back to Mississippi when he was promoting Gulf Coast shrimp. Of course, I tried it—and made my own version to serve at the restaurant for lunch. I would only prepare 10–12, and always secretly hoped some would not be ordered, so we could enjoy them for supper!

¾ cup fresh bread crumbs

1 tablespoon finely chopped parsley

2 tablespoons finely chopped garlic

½ teaspoon dried thyme

2 pounds eggplant (4–5 cups, cubed)

3 tablespoons flour

⅛ teaspoon salt

⅛ teaspoon finely ground black pepper

¾ cup olive oil, divided

3 cups diced tomatoes, drained

1½ pounds fresh raw medium shrimp, shelled and deveined

1) Preheat oven to 375°. In small bowl, combine bread crumbs, parsley, garlic, and thyme; mix well. Set aside.

2) Trim and discard ends of eggplant, then peel and cut eggplant into 1-inch cubes.

3) Mix flour with salt and black pepper, then dredge eggplant cubes in flour. Set aside.

4) Heat ⅓ cup oil in skillet, and when piping hot, add half the eggplant. Cook, stirring, until browned. Drain on paper towels; add more oil, and cook remaining eggplant; keep warm. Reserve oil in skillet.

5) Cook tomatoes in a saucepan 5 minutes on medium heat. Sprinkle lightly with salt and black pepper. Keep warm.

6) In skillet, heat reserved olive oil; add shrimp; sprinkle lightly with salt and black pepper; cook just until shrimp turn pink.

7) Divide eggplant into 6 au gratin dishes. Divide shrimp and tomato on each. Sprinkle crumb mixture on top. Drizzle 1 teaspoon olive oil over each. Bake 10–15 minutes, then run briefly under broiler to glaze.

143

LEMON BUTTER SEAFOOD

SERVES 6.

We used this recipe on a trip to New York in 2001 to promote U.S. Farm-Raised Catfish to magazines, the Food Network, and local TV stations. It was simple to prepare on camera, because I had the fish marinated, then cooked it live so hosts were able to taste it straight out of the hot pan. Of course, I didn't use the shrimp in that presentation, since we were focused on our catfish. After the trips, a number of media groups toured the Delta and came to The Crown for lunch. An AP reporter happened onto one of our bridge parties and used that in his story about the uniqueness of the Mississippi Delta.

½ cup Worcestershire

⅓ cup fresh lemon juice

½ teaspoon cayenne pepper

4 drops Tabasco

½ teaspoon ground thyme

1 clove garlic, finely minced

6 fish fillets (catfish, trout, cod, tilapia, etc.)

½ pound medium shrimp, peeled, tails off

4–6 tablespoons unsalted butter

1) Whisk together in a bowl the Worcestershire, lemon juice, cayenne, Tabasco, thyme, and garlic.

2) Place fish fillets and shrimp in large flat pan. Drizzle Worcestershire mixture over, lifting fillets to coat bottom. Marinate refrigerated at least 1 hour, up to 4 hours.

3) When ready to serve, melt 4 tablespoons butter in large skillet over medium heat. Add fillets and shrimp, shaking pan gently to prevent sticking. Cook 2 minutes, adding more butter as needed. Pour marinade into skillet, and simmer slowly, spooning juices over top of fillets for 2 minutes. Turn off heat, cover, and let sit until ready to serve. Serve warm over pasta or rice, with the pan juices.

NOTE: The marinade can also be used to flavor fish fillets or shrimp skewers cooked on the grill. Marinate fish or skewers as directed, then baste with marinade as you cook.

Barbecued Shrimp New Orleans Style

SERVES 4.

New Orleans barbecued shrimp has nothing to do with traditional BBQ flavors. You don't have to keep the shells and heads on the shrimp if you don't want to bother with the mess created by peeling it at the table. Just be sure to scoop up every drop of the sauce.

1 stick unsalted butter

½ cup olive oil

Juice of 3 lemons

1 teaspoon garlic powder

2 bay leaves

1 tablespoon chopped parsley

½ teaspoon crushed oregano leaves

2 teaspoons paprika

2 tablespoons Tabasco

1 tablespoon Worcestershire

1 teaspoon salt

1 teaspoon freshly ground black pepper

2 pounds medium or large shrimp, unpeeled, heads on

1) Melt butter in saucepan. Turn off heat, add remaining ingredients except shrimp, and mix well for 1 minute. Set sauce aside a few minutes for flavors to blend, or refrigerate overnight.

2) Wash shrimp, and place in large pot or Dutch oven. Warm sauce, if needed, and slowly pour over shrimp, touching as many as possible. Stir shrimp gently to coat well.

3) Cover, and cook on medium heat 15–20 minutes.

4) Serve immediately in bowls, with all the sauce, and a good, crusty bread for dipping.

TIDBIT: We've eaten this shrimp dish all over Louisiana, and loved every single version. Make a salad while the shrimp are cooking, and serve bread pudding for dessert. Laissez les bon temps roule! "Let the good times roll!"

SHRIMP AND GRITS

SERVES 4.

We have eaten Shrimp and Grits all over the South...from Charleston to Savannah to New Orleans, and everywhere in between. This recipe is our own version of this southern classic. Be sure to have French bread on hand for sopping up the juices.

SEAFOOD

5 slices bacon, finely diced

1 bunch green onions, sliced

1 green bell pepper, diced

2 cloves garlic, finely minced

1 stick unsalted butter

1½ pounds medium shrimp, shelled

6 ounces fresh mushrooms, thinly sliced

½ cup finely diced, unpeeled tomatoes

Juice of 1 lemon

4 drops Tabasco

½ teaspoon coarsely ground black pepper

½–1 cup dry white wine

Salt to taste

1) Cook bacon in large heavy skillet on medium heat, stirring until it starts to brown. Add onions, bell pepper, and garlic, stirring constantly 1 minute. Add butter, stirring to melt; scrape skillet.

2) Add shrimp, and cook, tossing and stirring, until shrimp barely turn pink. Add mushrooms, and continue to stir and toss until mushrooms begin to give up their juices.

3) Reduce heat to simmer; add tomatoes, lemon juice, Tabasco, black pepper, and ½ cup wine; mix well. Simmer 2–3 minutes.

4) Serve in a bowl poured over plain cooked grits or Delta Cheese Grits (page 95), so all the juices are captured and enjoyed.

Shrimp and Grits

CORN AND SHRIMP CASSEROLE

SERVES 4.

This is my variation of a Charleston shrimp and corn pie. It is wonderful for a Sunday night supper. I've also made it with catfish (of course), and with diced ham. Superb!

SEAFOOD

Sliced French bread, toasted

1 pound fresh shrimp, peeled, tails off

3 eggs

1 (15-ounce) can whole-kernel corn, drained

1½ cups milk

½ cup minced onion

½ cup minced green bell pepper

½ cup minced red bell pepper

½ teaspoon salt

1 tablespoon Worcestershire

2 teaspoons prepared mustard

½ teaspoon white pepper

1) Toast enough slices of bread to cover bottom of buttered 9x9-inch baking dish. Line dish with bread, and place shrimp evenly on top of bread. Set aside.

2) Place eggs in a bowl, and beat well. Add corn, milk, onion, both bell peppers, salt, Worcestershire, mustard, and white pepper, and mix thoroughly.

3) Pour corn mixture over shrimp. Cover loosely with aluminum foil. Bake in preheated 325° oven 1 hour or until set.

TIDBIT: Don't ever be afraid to make changes in any recipe. You may come up with something new and wonderful. (Just remember to write down what you did.) Recipe books are simply guides; if you don't have red bell pepper, use green; if you don't have wine, add a bit of lemon juice. Don't be afraid; just get in the kitchen, and have fun.

WANDA'S EASY CRAWFISH ÉTOUFFÉE

SERVES 6.

There are lots of complicated ways to make this luscious Louisiana specialty, but Wanda's recipe, dating from the time she lived there, tastes wonderful...and it's so quick!

1 stick unsalted butter

1 (16-ounce) package frozen crawfish tails

1 green bell pepper, chopped

1 onion, chopped

5 ribs fresh celery, chopped finely

2 (10-ounce) cans Rotel tomatoes

2 (10-ounce) cans cream of mushroom soup

1) In a large pan on medium heat, melt butter. Add crawfish tails, bell pepper, onion, and celery, and sauté 10 minutes.

2) Add Rotel and soup, and combine thoroughly. Turn heat to low, and cook about 45 minutes, stirring frequently.

3) Serve immediately, or cool and refrigerate until ready to serve. Étouffée can be held overnight, and warmed slowly to serve.

4) Serve over rice.

SEAFOOD

Delta Crawfish Boil

SERVES 6–8.

A crawfish boil is getting to be almost as popular as a catfish fry. People are cooking them outside in big frying pots, and even have special tables with a hole in the middle and a garbage can underneath so the crawfish can be dumped directly on the table. Everyone gathers around the table to eat, and throws the shells in the middle.

SEAFOOD

6–8 pounds fresh crawfish

1 large box crab boil

1–2 bags boiling onions, peeled

1 pound new potatoes, washed

8 pieces frozen corn on the cob, thawed

TIDBIT: In Louisiana, fresh artichokes and mushrooms are also added at times, and Jennifer loves those with crawfish. If desired, add the artichokes with the potatoes and the mushrooms with the crawfish.

1) Wash crawfish several times in water. Place a huge pot on the stove, fill halfway with water, and add crab boil spices. Bring to a boil.

2) Add onions and potatoes, and boil 10 minutes.

3) Add crawfish and corn, bring back to a boil; boil for 5 minutes. Turn heat off, and let sit in the spicy water a few minutes.

4) Lift crawfish and vegetables out of pot onto big pan to drain.

5) Transfer onto serving platters, put on table (cover table with paper to catch the drippings), and start eating—pulling off the heads, squeezing the tails, and enjoying every bite!

CAKES

Italian Cream Cake

Banana Cake with Creamy Caramel Icing

SERVES 12–15.

This luscious fresh banana cake dripping with rich caramel icing is just so darn delicious! Get the kids to help mash bananas, beat the icing, and make it a family affair.

CAKES

2½ cups sifted cake flour

2½ teaspoons baking powder

½ teaspoon baking soda

¾ teaspoon salt

½ teaspoon nutmeg

½ cup Crisco shortening or butter

1¼ cups sugar

3 eggs

1 teaspoon vanilla

1½ cups mashed ripe bananas (4–5)

CREAMY CARAMEL ICING:

2 cups sugar

1 teaspoon baking soda

¾ cup butter

½ cup buttermilk

1 tablespoon light corn syrup

12 large marshmallows

1 teaspoon vanilla

1) In a bowl, combine flour, baking powder, baking soda, salt, and nutmeg. Set aside.

2) In an electric mixing bowl, beat shortening until creamy; add sugar gradually, beating until batter is fluffy. Add eggs, one at a time, beating well after each addition.

3) Stir in vanilla; then add flour mixture alternately with bananas, beating after each addition, until batter is smooth. Pour into 2 greased and floured 9-inch cake pans.

4) Bake in preheated 375° oven about 25 minutes or until tester comes out clean. Cool cake completely before icing.

5) For icing, cook sugar, baking soda, butter, buttermilk, and syrup in large heavy saucepan over medium low heat, stirring constantly until smooth. Stir in marshmallows, and continue cooking until candy thermometer reaches 238°.

6) Transfer pan to counter padded with a towel. Add vanilla; beat until cloudy and of spreading consistency. This takes a little time, but is worth the effort.

7) Immediately ice cake. Holds well 2–3 days—but rarely lasts that long.

Fresh Carrot Cake

SERVES 12–15.

Homemade carrot cake is a celebration at our house, and it tastes so much better than store-bought cakes. Grate by hand, use a food processor, or mince carrot sticks from the store. However you prepare them, do bake this marvelous moist cake, and carry on the carrot cake tradition.

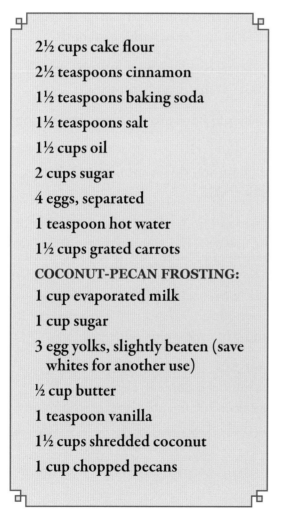

2½ cups cake flour

2½ teaspoons cinnamon

1½ teaspoons baking soda

1½ teaspoons salt

1½ cups oil

2 cups sugar

4 eggs, separated

1 teaspoon hot water

1½ cups grated carrots

COCONUT-PECAN FROSTING:

1 cup evaporated milk

1 cup sugar

3 egg yolks, slightly beaten (save whites for another use)

½ cup butter

1 teaspoon vanilla

1½ cups shredded coconut

1 cup chopped pecans

1) In a bowl, combine flour, cinnamon, baking soda, and salt. Set aside.

2) In an electric mixing bowl, cream oil with sugar until well mixed. Add 4 egg yolks, hot water, and carrots; continue mixing.

3) Slowly add flour mixture, and mix well. Beat egg whites, and gently fold in until thoroughly mixed.

4) Lightly grease and flour 2 (9-inch) cake pans, or a 9x13-inch baking pan. Pour batter into pans and bake in preheated 350° oven 30–50 minutes, depending on pan size, or until cake tester comes out clean in center. Cool before frosting.

5) For frosting, in saucepan over medium heat, combine milk, sugar, egg yolks, butter, and vanilla. Cook, stirring, until mixture is thickened, about 12 minutes. Add coconut and pecans, and mix well.

6) Cool until thick enough to spread, beating occasionally. Makes 2½ cups.

BOURBON NUT CAKE

SERVES 12–15.

Looks like a pound cake, cuts like a pound cake, but it is definitely more than a pound cake! It is wonderfully rich, lightly spicy, and packed with nuts, but not overly sweet. It's just right!

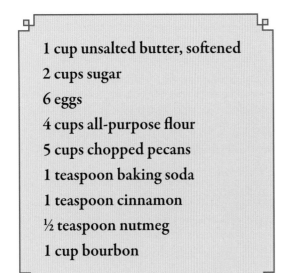

1 cup unsalted butter, softened

2 cups sugar

6 eggs

4 cups all-purpose flour

5 cups chopped pecans

1 teaspoon baking soda

1 teaspoon cinnamon

½ teaspoon nutmeg

1 cup bourbon

TIDBIT: We keep desserts on the Welsh dresser in the dining room from Thanksgiving on, with plates and napkins, ready for anyone who drops in to have a bite of something sweet. Tony loves this cake, and I can always tell when he's been nibbling because the cake keeps shrinking.

1) With electric mixer, cream butter and sugar together until fluffy. Beat in eggs, one at a time, until batter is smooth.

2) In a bowl, combine flour, pecans, baking soda, cinnamon, and nutmeg.

3) Slowly add flour mixture to batter, mixing until combined.

4) Add bourbon slowly into this stiff batter, stirring well.

5) Butter and flour a large tube pan or Bundt pan, and spoon batter into pan. Place into a pan of water on lower shelf of oven.

6) Bake in preheated 275° oven 2 hours, or until done, when a tester inserted in middle of cake comes out clean.

7) Cool cake, and invert onto cake plate; store under a dome to keep moist. If cake does become dry, drizzle with more bourbon. Cake keeps well for 1 week.

THE CROWN'S APPLE CAKE

SERVES 15–18.

One of my make-it-again cakes any time of the year. It's quick to prepare, and stays moist for days. We eat it for breakfast, and with ice cream for dessert.

2½ cups all-purpose flour

2 cups sugar

2 teaspoons baking powder

1 teaspoon baking soda

1 teaspoon salt

1 teaspoon cinnamon

1 teaspoon nutmeg

3 eggs, beaten

1 cup oil

1 teaspoon vanilla

3 cups chopped apples (peeled or unpeeled)

1) In a large bowl, combine flour, sugar, baking powder, baking soda, salt, cinnamon, and nutmeg; mix well.

2) Add beaten eggs, oil, and vanilla, and combine thoroughly. (This is a very stiff batter.)

3) Add apples, and stir vigorously to combine well. Pour batter into lightly oiled 9x13-inch baking pan.

4) Bake in preheated 325° oven about 50 minutes.

5) Apple cake does not need to be refrigerated; it will stay moist and delicious for a week.

TIDBIT: I prefer peelings left on the apples for texture, but peeled is fine.

PUMPKIN VARIATION: This recipe, using a small can of pumpkin instead of apples, makes a wonderfully moist Pumpkin Bread. Bake in sprayed loaf pans, small or large, 30–40 minutes. Keep an eye on them, and be sure middle of loaf has risen and is firm. Pumpkin Bread freezes perfectly and make a lovely gift.

CAKES

MISSISSIPPI MUD CAKE

SERVES 10–12.

Dense, dark, and superbly rich—a total chocolate experience. I love to serve this for dinner parties or to grandchildren on Sunday afternoon. The little bit of coffee in the batter makes the chocolate more intensely delicious! The Mud Bites variation is my favorite pick-up dessert when I'm planning a party, so take my advice—bake this cake!

1 cup melted butter

1 cup sugar

1 cup packed light brown sugar

¾ cup cocoa

¼ teaspoon salt

1 cup all-purpose flour

3 eggs, beaten

1 tablespoon coffee or water

CAKES

MUD BITES VARIATION: Bake batter in lightly buttered 8x12-inch pan, about 18 minutes. When ready to serve, cut into bite-size rectangles. I like to rub the top of the totally cold Mud Bites with powdered sugar, in a fairly deep layer, after they are cut, but are still in the pan. The dark and light makes a nice contrast, and they are a delicious bite of chocolate!

1) Place melted butter in large bowl. Add both sugars, and mix well. Add cocoa, salt, flour, eggs, and coffee, stirring vigorously to mix well.

2) Lightly butter a 9-inch round cake pan, line with parchment paper, then lightly butter paper. Pour batter into pan, and smooth onto sides evenly. Bake in preheated 350° oven 20–25 minutes. Do not overbake. Look for sides of cake to begin to pull away from pan. Cake should be set and seem dry to touch, but without a crust around edge.

3) Cool completely in pan, then turn cake onto serving plate, and cut into wedges, just like the ones at great bakeries. Garnish with whipped cream, ice cream, or fresh strawberries. Cut in thin slices.

Mississippi Mud Cake (above) and Mud Bites (below)

MUD PIE CHOCOLATE CAKE

SERVES 4–6.

Sometimes the simplest things taste absolutely wonderful. Children love making this mud pie cake, and it bakes so quickly they don't get impatient!

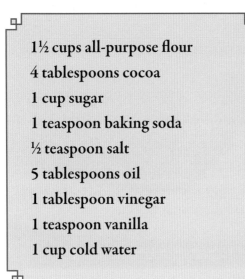

- 1½ cups all-purpose flour
- 4 tablespoons cocoa
- 1 cup sugar
- 1 teaspoon baking soda
- ½ teaspoon salt
- 5 tablespoons oil
- 1 tablespoon vinegar
- 1 teaspoon vanilla
- 1 cup cold water

1) In a bowl, thoroughly combine flour, cocoa, sugar, baking soda, and salt.

2) Butter a 9x9-inch square cake pan really well. Pour flour mixture evenly into buttered pan. Make 3 holes in flour mixture. Into one hole, pour oil, into another, the vinegar, into the third, the vanilla.

3) Then pour water over entire pan. Stir thoroughly with a spoon until you can't see the flour. (Kids love this mud pie part.)

4) Bake in preheated 350° oven 30 minutes. Cut into squares, and serve with ice cream.

TIDBIT: At the library in Ubon, Thailand, I found Peg Bracken's *I Hate To Cook Book*. I loved reading her funny stories, and learned a lot from her simple, practical ways of entertaining. We only had a charcoal hibachi and a tiny toaster oven at the time, so this recipe to make a real cake using just a spoon was a gift beyond belief, and I made it often. Until then, the only dessert we had was from a child who came by once a week carrying a woven tray of small cakes balanced on his head. I always bought a bunch from the "muffin boy," and made a glaze with orange juice and sugar to "ice" the muffins. We had to get creative in Thailand in 1965.

CAKES

CRAZY DELTA CHOCOLATE CAKE

SERVES 12–15.

Great recipes are passed from generation to generation and enjoyed all along the way. Crazy Delta Chocolate Cake is a special recipe, passed along to me by Isabel Hamilton Hernandez. This cake is dense, moist, and absolutely addictive.

CAKES

2 cups sugar

2 cups all-purpose flour

½ teaspoon salt

4 tablespoons cocoa

½ cup oil

1 stick unsalted butter

1 cup water

2 eggs, beaten, at room temperature

1 teaspoon vanilla

½ cup buttermilk

1 teaspoon baking soda

CRAZY ICING:

1 stick unsalted butter

6 tablespoons milk

4 tablespoons cocoa

1 (1-pound) box confectioners' sugar

1 teaspoon vanilla

1 cup chopped pecans

1) In large mixing bowl, sift together sugar, flour, salt, and cocoa, and mix well.

2) In saucepan, bring oil, butter, and water to a boil. Pour hot liquid over flour mixture, and combine thoroughly. Add beaten eggs and vanilla, and mix well.

3) Whisk together buttermilk and baking soda. Add to batter, and combine all ingredients thoroughly.

4) Pour into buttered 9x13-inch cake pan. Bake in preheated 350° oven about 25 minutes.

5) Remove cake from oven, and let cool slightly while icing is prepared.

6) For Crazy Icing, in a large saucepan, bring butter, milk, and cocoa to a boil, stirring constantly. Add powdered sugar and vanilla, mixing well.

7) Then stir in pecans, and pour over warm cake. Set aside to cool completely. Cake will hold well 2–3 days if you can stay out of it.

BEVERLY'S PERFECT POUND CAKE

SERVES 10–12.

Beverly Adams makes a pound cake for every family gathering, and one of her cakes has been our Christmas present for years, a treasured gift. Once, when we missed a family get together, Beverly mailed me the last two pieces of cake left that day in a little box!

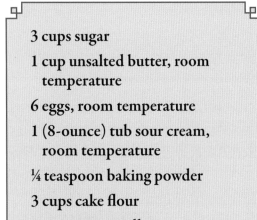

3 cups sugar

1 cup unsalted butter, room temperature

6 eggs, room temperature

1 (8-ounce) tub sour cream, room temperature

¼ teaspoon baking powder

3 cups cake flour

1 teaspoon vanilla

Flour for dusting pan

TIP: To make your pound cake release with no sticking, melt 2–3 tablespoons of shortening to generously paint the complete inside of pan before adding batter. Cake won't stick at all.

NOTE: It is very important that butter, eggs, and sour cream are at room temperature.

1) Cream sugar and butter with an electric mixer until fluffy. Add eggs, one at a time, mixing until well blended before adding next egg. Add sour cream, and blend well.

2) Stir baking powder into flour. Slowly mix flour mixture, 1 cup at a time, into egg mixture. Add vanilla, and mix again.

3) Butter a Bundt or tube pan well, and dust with flour. Pour batter into pan, and bake in preheated 325° oven 1 hour and 15 minutes.

4) Cool cake on rack 15 minutes, then invert onto serving plate. Serve warm or cold. Cake keeps well for several days, tightly covered.

TIP: If you can resist eating the entire cake while it's warm, a pound cake can be frozen for several weeks. Wrap cake tightly in foil, then place in a freezer bag. Your cake will wait patiently until you just have to have a bite of something sweet!

CAKES

Beverly's Perfect Pound Cake

Sage's Christmas Coconut Cake

SERVES 10–12.

My grandchildren are a joy to have helping in the kitchen, especially at Christmastime. Sage particularly likes the delicious details of desserts and always makes lots of them. Coconut Cake at Christmas is a family tradition.

1 (18¼-ounce) box cake mix, butter recipe (white or yellow)

1 (16-ounce) tub whipped topping

1 (16-ounce) carton sour cream

3 packages frozen shredded coconut, thawed

1 cup packaged dry coconut to garnish

1) Prepare cake mix according to directions on the box. Pour batter into 2 (9-inch) round cake pans that have been sprayed and dusted with a little flour.

2) Bake as directed on box. Cool completely. When cool, turn cakes out onto 2 cookie sheets. Using a long bread knife, slice evenly through the sides forming 4 layers.

3) In a large bowl, mix whipped topping, sour cream, and thawed coconut, folding until frosting is well mixed.

4) Place 1 cake layer on cake plate, spread frosting evenly, and continue with remaining layers. Spread frosting on sides and over top.

5) Sprinkle dry coconut on top, and press lightly into sides. Refrigerate 2–3 days before serving. Cake keeps well for several days after cutting.

COFFEE WALNUT CAKE

SERVES 10-12.

This traditional cake is served in tea rooms and homes all over the British Isles. The coffee flavor is intense because of the coffee syrup used in the icing and cake. In England, we could buy Camp Coffee, a liquid coffee syrup used in the colonies and on army campaigns when a cup of coffee was desired, but coffee couldn't be brewed properly. I suppose it was the first "instant coffee." I often double the syrup and keep it in the freezer, because I make this cake often—and love every bite.

5 tablespoons instant coffee

5 tablespoons boiling water

1 (18¼-ounce) box butter or yellow cake mix

3 eggs

⅓ cup oil

1¼ cups cold coffee (left from that morning is fine)

COFFEE CREAM ICING:

4 ounces unsalted butter, softened

1 (1-pound) box confectioners' sugar

1 cup chopped walnuts

1) Preheat oven to 350°. Combine instant coffee and hot water, stirring until dissolved, to make 5 tablespoons coffee syrup to be used in cake and icing.

2) Prepare cake mix as directed on box, using eggs, oil, coffee (instead of water), and 2 tablespoons of the coffee syrup.

3) Bake as directed on box in 2 (9-inch) cake pans that have been buttered and dusted with flour. Cool before icing.

4) For icing, in mixing bowl, beat butter with remaining 3 tablespoons coffee syrup. Slowly add sugar, beating until fairly stiff. For a softer icing, add a bit of cold coffee or milk until desired consistency is reached. Ice cake, and sprinkle walnuts on top.

TIP: The taste is even better when made 2–3 days in advance, and it freezes well.

VARIATION: Cake can also be baked in a 9x13-inch pan, and iced in one layer. I like to make tiny individual cakes in mini muffin pans, then ice each cake separately, and top with chopped walnuts or a walnut half.

CAKES

ITALIAN CREAM CAKE

SERVES 8-10.

When I first tasted this cake at a church potluck supper, I immediately fell in love with it! Now I make it for family birthdays, weddings, anniversaries, and just any time we get hungry for this luscious cake!

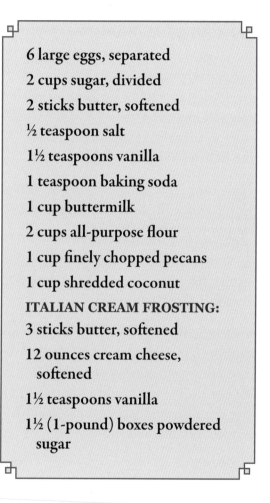

6 large eggs, separated

2 cups sugar, divided

2 sticks butter, softened

½ teaspoon salt

1½ teaspoons vanilla

1 teaspoon baking soda

1 cup buttermilk

2 cups all-purpose flour

1 cup finely chopped pecans

1 cup shredded coconut

ITALIAN CREAM FROSTING:

3 sticks butter, softened

12 ounces cream cheese, softened

1½ teaspoons vanilla

1½ (1-pound) boxes powdered sugar

1) In electric mixing bowl, beat egg whites until soft peaks form. Slowly beat in ½ cup sugar until stiff peaks form. Transfer mixture into another bowl.

2) In original mixing bowl, cream butter, remaining 1½ cups sugar, salt, and vanilla. Beat in egg yolks one at a time, until consistency of whipped cream.

3) Stir baking soda into buttermilk. Add alternately with flour to butter mixture, beginning and ending with flour. Fold in egg whites, then add pecans and coconut (using slow speed on mixer, or by hand).

4) Pour batter into 3 (9-inch) cake pans that have been buttered and floured. Bake in preheated 325° oven about 40 minutes. Cool cakes, and remove from pans.

5) For frosting, combine butter, cream cheese, and vanilla in electric mixing bowl, until smooth. Slowly add sugar, and continue beating until smooth and creamy.

6) Frost layers and sides of cooled cake. Refrigerate iced cake.

CAKES

COOKIES & CANDIES

Mint Chocolate Squares

No-Bake Chocolate Oatmeal Cookies

MAKES 2–3 DOZEN.

Since no hot pans are coming hot out of the oven for this recipe, let the kids stir and dip the cookies on their own. I know it's got sugar in it, but it's mostly oatmeal, and so delicious that I still call it a "healthy cookie."

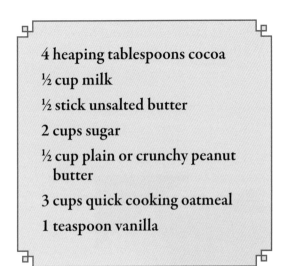

4 heaping tablespoons cocoa

½ cup milk

½ stick unsalted butter

2 cups sugar

½ cup plain or crunchy peanut butter

3 cups quick cooking oatmeal

1 teaspoon vanilla

1) In a large saucepan, bring cocoa, milk, butter, and sugar to a boil, stirring frequently. Let boil for only 1 minute, then remove from heat.

2) Stir in peanut butter until melted. Add oatmeal and vanilla, stirring vigorously until mixture is combined thoroughly.

3) Drop cookie mixture onto wax paper. Allow cookies to cool completely before eating (if you can keep the kids out of them).

PEANUT BUTTER COOKIES

MAKES 5–6 DOZEN.

My grandmother and I made these together often when I was growing up. My job was pushing the fork onto the cookie to make the pattern. As I got older, Momo would let me mix and roll as well. We would bake cookies, then have a tea party on the porch or on the grass on my little table.

1 cup sugar

1 cup packed brown sugar

¾ cup shortening, melted

¾ cup peanut butter

2 eggs, well beaten

2 teaspoons vanilla

3 cups all-purpose flour

¾ teaspoon salt

1 teaspoon baking soda

1) In large mixing bowl, thoroughly combine both sugars with melted shortening and peanut butter. Stir in eggs and vanilla.

2) In another bowl, mix flour, salt, and baking soda.

3) Add flour mixture to peanut butter mixture, and stir vigorously until dough is well mixed. Chill dough 1–2 hours.

4) Pinch off small pieces of cookie dough, roll into balls, and place on lightly sprayed cookie sheets.

5) Flatten each cookie with the tines of a fork, making a criss-cross pattern. Bake in preheated 400° oven 8–10 minutes.

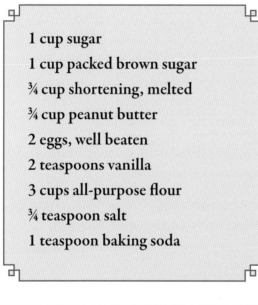

LEMON CHEESECAKE TRIANGLES

MAKES 36.

These bite-size cheesecakes are simply addictive—they round out many a menu perfectly.

⅓ cup packed light brown sugar

1 cup all-purpose flour

½ cup chopped pecans or walnuts

⅔ stick unsalted butter, melted

1 (8-ounce) package cream cheese, softened

¼ cup sugar

1 egg, beaten

2 tablespoons milk

1½ tablespoons lemon juice

½ teaspoon grated lemon rind

1 teaspoon vanilla

⅓ cup fine graham cracker crumbs

1) Preheat oven to 350°. In a small bowl, mix together brown sugar, flour, pecans, and butter until well mixed and crumbly. Press mixture into sprayed 9x13-inch pan, and bake 12–15 minutes until firm and lightly browned. Cool crust.

2) In an electric mixing bowl, beat cream cheese, sugar, egg, milk, lemon juice, lemon rind, and vanilla until smooth. Pour mixture over cold crust.

3) Sprinkle with graham cracker crumbs, and bake about 20 minutes until set.

4) Cool on wire rack. Cut in 2-inch squares, then in half to make small triangles.

CHOCOLATE CHIP BARS

MAKES ABOUT 40.

Everyone loves these! They are more moist than a chocolate chip cookie, and don't crumble as easily, so they are perfect for parties, picnics, tailgating, and school lunches. For Afternoon Tea at The Crown, we cut them in squares, and top them with a dollop of whipped cream and a dusting of finely chopped pecans.

2 sticks unsalted butter, softened

¾ cup sugar

¾ cup packed brown sugar

1 teaspoon vanilla

2 eggs

2¼ cups all-purpose flour

1 teaspoon baking soda

1 teaspoon salt

2 cups chocolate chips

1 cup chopped pecans or walnuts

1) In an electric mixing bowl, combine butter, sugar, brown sugar, and vanilla, mixing until creamy. Add eggs, one at a time, beating well after each addition.

2) Mix flour, baking soda, and salt, then slowly add flour mixture to batter until well combined.

3) Stir in chocolate chips and pecans until thoroughly mixed, and pour into lightly buttered 10x15-inch baking pan.

4) Bake in preheated 375° oven 20–25 minutes. Cool, and cut into rectangles. Bars will keep well several days, and can be frozen.

ANGELIC COCONUT PECAN SLICES

MAKES ABOUT 48.

I started making these tasty bites when we lived in England. I didn't have pecans, so I used all coconut instead. The fresh lemony topping sets the sweet filling off perfectly—and I do love the pecans!

CRUST:

1 stick unsalted butter, softened

¼ cup sugar

1 egg

1¼ cups all-purpose flour

⅛ teaspoon salt

½ teaspoon vanilla

FILLING:

2 eggs, beaten

1½ cups packed brown sugar

½ cup flaked coconut

1 cup chopped pecans

2 tablespoons all-purpose flour

½ teaspoon baking powder

½ teaspoon salt

1 teaspoon vanilla

1½ cups confectioners' sugar, sifted

Juice of 2 lemons

1) In electric mixing bowl, cream together butter and sugar. Beat egg in well.

2) Mix flour and salt; add to butter mixture in 3 stages; mix in vanilla.

3) Place mixture in lightly buttered 9x13-inch pan. Smooth evenly in pan. Bake in preheated 350° oven 12–15 minutes.

4) For Filling, thoroughly combine eggs, sugar, coconut, pecans, flour, baking powder, salt, and vanilla. Spread mixture on baked crust; return to oven 20–25 minutes. Cool.

5) Put confectioners' sugar in bowl, and gradually add enough lemon juice to make a good spreading consistency.

6) Spread on cooled cookie; cut into small rectangles. Keeps for days and freezes well.

COOKIES

170

Mint Chocolate Squares

MAKES 80–100 BITES.

CAKE LAYER:

6 (1-ounce) squares unsweetened baking chocolate

1½ sticks butter

6 eggs

3 cups sugar

1½ cups all-purpose flour

1 cup chopped pecans (optional)

MINT LAYER:

1 stick plus 1 tablespoon butter, softened

4½ cups powdered sugar

6 tablespoons whipping cream or evaporated milk

2–3 teaspoons peppermint extract

1–3 drops green food coloring

CHOCOLATE TOPPING:

4–5 tablespoons butter

12 ounces chocolate chips

1 teaspoon vanilla

1) Melt chocolate squares and butter in saucepan. Set aside to cool.

2) In an electric mixing bowl, beat eggs and sugar until thick. Stir in flour, chocolate mixture, and pecans, if desired.

3) Pour batter into lightly buttered 9x13-inch metal pan, spreading evenly. Bake in preheated 350° oven 25 minutes. Set aside to completely cool in pan.

4) For Mint Layer, mix butter and sugar, adding cream and peppermint; mix in food coloring. Spread over cold Cake; chill 1 hour.

5) For Topping, slowly heat 2 tablespoons butter in saucepan. Stir in chocolate chips until melted, adding more butter, if needed. Remove from heat, and stir in vanilla until mixture is shiny and smooth.

6) Drizzle over cold Mint Layer in decorative pattern, or smooth out over entire pan. Cover, and chill 1 hour before cutting into squares with knife dipped in hot water. Can refrigerate 3 days.

Tip: Mint squares freeze perfectly for four weeks in the pan, or after they have been cut, kept tightly wrapped in plastic containers.

MAMA'S MARSHMALLOW BROWNIES

MAKES ABOUT 12.

These are gooey and rich, and sometimes you just have to eat them out of the pan with a spoon, because you can't wait for them to get cool! Great to take, especially if you want to have the most popular dish at the party! Just plan on eating them with a fork...these are not finger food!

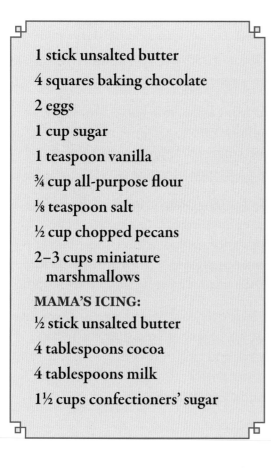

1 stick unsalted butter

4 squares baking chocolate

2 eggs

1 cup sugar

1 teaspoon vanilla

¾ cup all-purpose flour

⅛ teaspoon salt

½ cup chopped pecans

2–3 cups miniature
    marshmallows

MAMA'S ICING:

½ stick unsalted butter

4 tablespoons cocoa

4 tablespoons milk

1½ cups confectioners' sugar

1) In small saucepan on medium heat, melt butter. Add chocolate, and stir constantly until chocolate melts; set aside.

2) In large bowl, beat eggs with sugar, then vanilla. Add chocolate mixture, stirring until completely mixed. Add flour and salt, stirring to combine, then stir in pecans.

3) Pour mixture into well-buttered 9x13-inch baking dish, and smooth to edges. Bake in preheated 350° oven 30 minutes.

4) Completely cover brownie with marshmallows, and return to oven 1–2 minutes, just long enough for marshmallows to melt, but not brown. Let brownies cool just slightly.

5) For icing, mix all ingredients well, then spread over warm cake. Run a knife through the icing and melted marshmallows for a decorative pattern.

Mama's Marshmallow Brownies

SOUTHERN PECAN PRALINES

MAKES 30-40.

Pralines are the South's favorite candy. Anyone in our family returning from a visit to New Orleans always brings pralines to those of us who couldn't go. Jennifer was living in New Orleans when she married, and pralines were on platters at the reception. I remember many times making the pralines when it was a bit damp or hot, and just praying that the pieces would harden. They always do, but sometimes it takes a little extra time. Now when I make pralines, I just start out praying over them!

1⅓ cups unsalted sugar

⅔ cup packed brown sugar

⅔ cup water

⅔ teaspoon vinegar

⅛ teaspoon salt

¼ teaspoon cream of tartar

3 tablespoons unsalted butter

2 cups chopped pecans

1) In large, heavy pan, over low heat, combine sugar, brown sugar, water, vinegar, salt, and cream of tartar. Cover pot, and cook about 3 minutes so steam will dissolve any crystals from sides of pan. Uncover, and cook on medium high to a soft-ball stage. (236° on candy thermometer.) Test by dropping a few drops into cold water in a bowl to see if you can form a ball with your fingers.

2) Remove pan from heat, stir in butter, and beat by hand until candy begins to lose its gloss, and begins to thicken. Immediately stir in pecans.

3) Drop from a spoonful onto buttered wax paper or foil. Make any size you choose. (I prefer small ones, that I can eat in 2 or 3 bites.)

4) When fully hardened, store in wax-paper-lined tins or plastic containers with wax paper between each layer. To give as gifts, place a few pralines into small candy bags, and tie with a ribbon.

GRANNY'S MARTHA WASHINGTON BALLS

MAKES 8 DOZEN OR MORE.

Candy is such a tradition in families. My niece Katie has continued Granny's tradition, making these scrumptious candies every Christmas as gifts for everyone in the family to enjoy. Wonderful fun for the kids to help make, and a great gift!

1 stick unsalted butter, softened

2 (1-pound) boxes confectioners' sugar

4 cups finely chopped pecans

1 (14-ounce) bag shredded coconut

1 (14-ounce) can sweetened condensed milk

⅓ block paraffin wax (optional)

2 (12-ounce) bags chocolate chips

1) In large mixing bowl, cream butter and sugar well. Add pecans, coconut, and sweetened condensed milk, mixing all together completely. Refrigerate mixture until very cold, or overnight.

2) Shape into walnut-size balls, and place each on cookie sheet lined with wax paper. Place in freezer for several hours, until firm.

3) In top of double boiler, melt paraffin, if desired, according to box directions, adding chocolate chips and mixing well. Keep chocolate mixture warm in bowl of hot water while balls are being dipped. (Balls can be dipped in melted chocolate without using paraffin.)

4) Using a toothpick, dip each ball into melted chocolate, and set back on wax paper to cool. Remove toothpick, and dab chocolate over hole, if needed. Refrigerate balls until cold before removing to serving plate or airtight containers. Balls will hold well 2 weeks at room temperature.

WANDA'S FABULOUS FUDGE

MAKES 6 POUNDS.

My sister Wanda is the fudge maker in the family, and I think her less-fuss, updated version of old-fashioned fudge is truly wonderful.

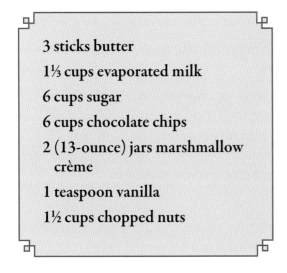

3 sticks butter

1⅓ cups evaporated milk

6 cups sugar

6 cups chocolate chips

2 (13-ounce) jars marshmallow crème

1 teaspoon vanilla

1½ cups chopped nuts

1) In a large heavy pan on medium heat, combine butter, milk, and sugar, stirring well to melt sugar. Bring mixture to a rolling boil, stirring constantly. Boil, stirring constantly, until temperature reaches 234° on candy thermometer, about 7 minutes. Mixture is ready when drops form a semi-hard ball in cold water.

2) Stir in chocolate chips and marshmallow crème until melted and combined well. Add vanilla and nuts, and mix well.

3) Pour into a large buttered pan, smoothing fudge to edges of pan. Cool at least 4 hours before cutting. Store in airtight container. Keeps well for several weeks.

TIDBIT: Mama always made the old-fashioned fudge, and it was heavenly... especially standing in the kitchen watching her stir and smelling that aroma, waiting for her to pour it out of the pot. Wanda's version has all the flavor, is a lot less time-consuming, and is our new family tradition.

CANDIES

PIES

Old-Fashioned Lemon Ice Box Pie

Mama's Fresh Strawberry Pie

SERVES 6–8.

We longed for this pie in the summer when fresh berries were in the market. Mama made it the day before she wanted to serve it, but it was hard to keep us out of it. Louisiana and Mississippi strawberries are the best, small and sweet and in season for such a short time. Daddy would make a run down to pick up berries, and then we were in heaven eating pies and strawberry shortcake to our heart's content.

1 cup sugar

3 tablespoons cornstarch

1 (3-ounce) box strawberry gelatin

1 cup warm water

½ teaspoon red food coloring, or more (optional)

3–4 cups halved small fresh strawberries

1 (9-inch) pie crust, baked

1 cup whipping cream, whipped, or Cool Whip

1) In a large saucepan, combine sugar, cornstarch, gelatin, water, and food coloring. Cook on medium heat until thick.

2) Cool slightly, and add strawberries, stirring well. Pour into baked pie crust.

3) Refrigerate 3–4 hours, or overnight. When ready to serve, top each slice with whipped cream.

OLD-FASHIONED LEMON ICE BOX PIE

SERVES 6–8.

LOVE this old-fashioned lemon pie! When it's in the refrigerator, I will open that door again and again for just one more sliver—until it's gone!

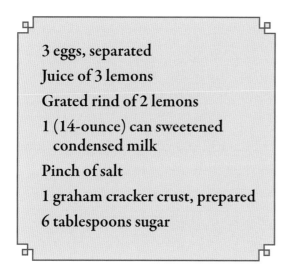

3 eggs, separated

Juice of 3 lemons

Grated rind of 2 lemons

1 (14-ounce) can sweetened condensed milk

Pinch of salt

1 graham cracker crust, prepared

6 tablespoons sugar

1) Place egg yolks in large bowl, and beat well with a spoon. Add lemon juice and rind, and continue to beat. Add sweetened condensed milk and salt, and mix thoroughly. Pour lemon mixture into crust.

2) Beat eggs whites with electric mixer until soft peaks form. Add sugar slowly, 2 tablespoons at a time, continuing to beat until all sugar is added, and stiff peaks form.

3) Place meringue carefully on top of pie, taking edge and covering all filling. Touch meringue gently with a spoon to form peaks all over top.

4) Bake in preheated 400°oven 4–5 minutes, until meringue is golden. Cool, then refrigerate.

Grammie Cameron's Apple Pie Recipe

SERVES 6–8.

Since Deanna and Kevin married, I've been fascinated with the Apple Pie Contest and got to enter one year when we joined them for Thanksgiving. Carter and Izabela are fierce competitors too, so they make three pies at their house, lucky Kevin! Here's Deanna's story:

Mary Cameron was my mom's mom. Her house always felt like Thanksgiving. You were always greeted with smells of something delicious roasting or baking, and huge hugs from Grammie just for showing up. My mom's house is the same way, but especially so at Thanksgiving. It is a time for laughter, love...and cutthroat competitiveness!

Every year, my mom's side of the family gathers together on Thanksgiving evening and blindfolds some unsuspecting stranger—usually a neighbor or a new boyfriend—to taste test anywhere from a half-dozen to a dozen apple pies. When it is decided, the jubilant winner gets bragging rights until the next Thanksgiving!

When Grammie Cameron died way too young, in May of 1977, no one could bear the idea of the empty space where her pie would have been, so everyone made their own and brought it to my mom's house. There were five apple pies that year, from Mom, her sisters Irene, Ellie, Mary, and family friend Barbara Mock. Camerons being Scots, it became competitive immediately, and the tradition was born. Grandpa Dougald judged the contest (yes,

blindfolded) and my mother grudgingly admits that my Aunt Irene won that year.

Almost forty years later, we're still going strong. We're into our third generation of fabulous pie bakers and the judge is still blindfolded for this deliciously fun tradition.

> "Mom, each time I roll out my crust,
>   I experience a déjà vu.
> There's a feeling down inside of me that says:
>   Part of me is part of you."
>   —Mary Cameron Mundie (1983)

DOUBLE CRUST:

2 cups all-purpose flour

1 teaspoon salt

⅔ cup shortening, chilled, cut into ½-inch pieces

5–7 tablespoons ice water, divided

FILLING:

½ cup sugar

1 teaspoon cinnamon

½ teaspoon ground nutmeg

1 tablespoon all-purpose flour

8 apples (mix of Macintosh, Cortlands, Grannie Smiths), peeled, cored, and sliced thinly

1 tablespoon lemon juice

TO FINISH:

3 tablespoons unsalted butter, diced

1 tablespoon milk

Raw sugar to sprinkle

Izabela carries on the pie-making tradition.

1) Sift flour and salt into food processor bowl fitted with pastry blade. Add shortening and 5 tablespoons ice water. Pulse until dough starts to hold together; if necessary, add more ice water 1 tablespoon at a time, until dough starts to form a ball.

2) Divide into 2 portions, 1 slightly bigger than the other. On a floured surface, pat each portion into a disk shape. Wrap each in plastic wrap; chill at least 30 minutes. Dough can be made up to one month ahead and kept in freezer.) Prepare Filling while dough chills.

3) For Filling, in a large bowl, combine sugar, cinnamon, nutmeg, and flour. Add apples and lemon juice; stir and toss to coat.

4) Roll out smaller disk of dough on floured surface to about a 12-inch circle, and slightly overhang on pie plate.

5) Spoon apple mixture into crust. Pile up high in the middle, above plate rim; it will cook down quite a bit. Dot with butter.

6) Roll out second dough disk to about a 13-inch circle. Drape over apple mixture for top crust. Pinch crusts together, and fold edges under. Vent crust with decorative slashes; brush with milk; sprinkle with sugar. Chill 10 minutes.

7) Preheat oven to 400°. Place pie on baking sheet (to catch any spillage) on middle oven rack. Bake until crust begins to brown, about 20 minutes. Turn oven down to 350°, and continue baking until crust is a beautiful golden brown.

OLD-FASHIONED FRIED PEACH PIES

MAKES 12–14 PIES.

When Momo made fried pies, we never left the kitchen. As soon as they were cool enough to touch, we would grab a pie, take a tiny bite to test it, blow on it madly, and eat it while it was still really warm. These luscious pies ooze sweet peach filling when you bite through the crust, and three bites later, you grab another one!

1 (6-ounce) package dried peaches
½ cup sugar
1 teaspoon fresh lemon juice
2 cups water
Pinch of salt
1 package refrigerated pie crusts
Flour for dusting workspace
Milk or water for sealing dough
Oil for frying

TIP: Pies can be baked in preheated 425° oven 15–20 minutes.

1) Chop peaches, and place in a large saucepan. Stir in sugar, lemon juice, water, and salt, and bring to a boil. Reduce heat, and simmer until peaches are tender, about 30 minutes. Take off heat, and stir until fruit is mashed, and all liquid is absorbed. Set aside to cool.

2) Place 1 pie crust on lightly floured work surface, and with floured rolling pin, lightly roll out a little thinner. Using a bowl (about 5 inches) as a guide, cut as many circles as possible from crust.

3) Put about 2 tablespoons filling in center of each circle. Rub edge of pastry with milk, then fold over filling, making a half moon. Rub milk on edge of half circle, and turn fold in just a bit. Dip a fork in flour, and gently pat edge to seal. Use extra dough to cut additional circles.

4) In a large skillet, add oil to 1¼ inches in depth. When oil is hot, place 4–5 pies at a time in skillet; do not crowd. Cook until golden brown, turning very carefully just once. Remove; drain on paper towels.

MAGNOLIA MACAROON PIE

SERVES 6–8.

This reminds me of wonderful times at my grandmother's house. Everyone has food memories, and in the South, we cherish them all—because we love to eat!

1 stick unsalted butter

1½ cups sugar

¼ cup all-purpose flour

¼ teaspoon salt

½ cup water

2 eggs, beaten

1⅓ cups flaked coconut

1 unbaked pie crust

¼ cup chopped pecans or almonds (optional)

1) Melt butter in saucepan over low heat, or microwave in a bowl.

2) Stir in sugar, flour, salt, and water, and combine well.

3) Add eggs and coconut, mixing thoroughly.

4) Scatter pecans in pie shell, if desired, then pour coconut mixture into pie shell.

5) Bake in preheated 325° oven 45 minutes.

PIES

THE CROWN'S PLANTATION PIE

SERVES 6–8.

When The Crown was in the cotton fields, my Kentucky Derby Pie was a big favorite. As we began creating dry mixes for our Taste of Gourmet line of products, we couldn't use nuts, because of the short shelf life, and we couldn't call it Kentucky Derby! So the solution was to substitute coconut for the pecans, and call our own version Plantation Pie, which is now one of our best-selling mixes! I usually stop by the dessert table, pick up a piece of this pie, put it in a napkin, and eat it on the way out of The Crown...almost every day. Scrumptious!

1 cup sugar

½ cup all-purpose flour

1 stick unsalted butter, melted

2 eggs, beaten

1 cup flaked coconut (or chopped pecans)

1 teaspoon vanilla

1 tablespoon Kentucky bourbon (optional)

1 cup chocolate chips

1 unbaked pie crust

1) In a large bowl, mix sugar and flour with a spoon. Stir in melted butter, mixing well.

2) Add beaten eggs, and mix again.

3) Add coconut or pecans, vanilla, and bourbon, mixing well.

4) Touch batter; if it is cool, add chocolate chips. Do not add if batter is warm enough to melt chips.

5) Mix thoroughly, pour into pie crust, and bake in preheated 325° oven 40–45 minutes.

PIES

The Crown's Plantation Pie

AUNT MALLIE'S PECAN PIE

SERVES 6–8.

At Thanksgiving and Christmas I always bake my Aunt Mallie's Pecan Pie, and there's never a bite left. Pecans are abundant throughout the South, and served in lots of ways, but pecan pie is the ultimate southern dessert.

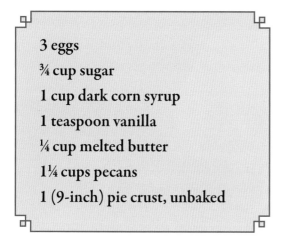

3 eggs

¾ cup sugar

1 cup dark corn syrup

1 teaspoon vanilla

¼ cup melted butter

1¼ cups pecans

1 (9-inch) pie crust, unbaked

1) In large bowl, beat eggs well. Add sugar, and beat well. Stir in syrup, vanilla, and butter, mixing thoroughly.

2) Coarsely chop pecans, if you choose, leaving a few in halves, or leave all pecans in halves. (Aunt Mallie chopped them all.) Put pecans in bottom of pie crust.

3) Stir syrup mixture again before pouring into pie crust. The pecans will come to the top of the pie.

4) Bake in preheated 350° oven 40–45 minutes. Let pie cool before cutting.

5) Pecan pie will keep for several days unrefrigerated, and can be frozen for 2 months.

TIDBIT: Growing up, the entire family spent Christmas Eve at Aunt Mallie and Uncle C.E. Powell's house for 35 years, until all the cousins married and started to take turns. They lived at Linn, in Sunflower County, on land the family had settled in the 1840's. Now, Christmas Eve is always at our house for friends and all the family who aren't obligated elsewhere. Christmas is my favorite time of the year, especially when our grandchildren, Sage and Prescott, are in the kitchen helping me with the cooking and special desserts.

PIES

DELTA PECAN TASSIES

MAKES 24.

These tiny pecan pies are a Delta favorite for pick-up desserts at cocktail parties, showers, and teas, with all the flavor of a full-size pecan pie, but none of the mess. I love pick-up desserts for a big party—miniature Pavlova, Mississippi Mud Bites, Chocolate Mint Squares, and small slices of Coffee Walnut Cake. Keep some in the freezer for snacking!

1 stick plus 2 tablespoons unsalted butter, softened, divided

3 ounces cream cheese, softened

1 cup all-purpose flour

1 cup pecans halves, divided

¾ cup packed light brown sugar

1 egg, beaten

1 teaspoon vanilla

Dash of salt

1) In a bowl, cream 1 stick butter with cream cheese.

2) Add flour, and work it in with your fingers. Roll dough into a ball, and chill. (This can be done a day ahead.)

3) When ready to bake, lightly spray or butter miniature muffin tins. Divide dough into 24 tiny balls, and press each one into a muffin tin and up the side a bit, making 24 tiny pastry shells.

4) Press 1 pecan half into bottom of each muffin tin. Chop remaining pecans, and set aside.

5) In a small bowl, combine sugar, egg, remaining 2 tablespoons butter, vanilla, and salt, and mix thoroughly. Spoon filling into each muffin tin, and top with chopped pecans.

6) Bake in preheated 325° oven 20–25 minutes, until light golden brown. Cool completely before removing from muffin tins.

7) Tassies will keep, tightly covered, for several days.

SOUTHERN PRALINE PIE WITH CARAMEL PECAN SAUCE

SERVES 6–8.

Dessert just doesn't get any better than this scrumptious pie served warm with ice cream and Caramel Pecan Sauce! Pralines are the South's favorite candy, and this pie captures that sugary crunch. Sauce is also great on ice cream and other desserts.

1 stick unsalted butter

⅓ cup plus 1 tablespoon sugar

1 cup packed dark brown sugar

⅓ cup all-purpose flour

¼ cup oatmeal

¼ teaspoon salt

½ teaspoon baking powder

1 teaspoon vanilla

2 eggs, beaten

½–1 cup chopped pecans (optional)

1 (9-inch) pie shell, unbaked

CARAMEL PECAN SAUCE:

⅓ cup dark brown sugar

⅓ cup hot water

1 cup light corn syrup

1 cup dark corn syrup

1 cup halved or chopped pecans

2 teaspoons vanilla

1) Melt butter in large bowl in microwave. Add sugar, brown sugar, flour, oatmeal, salt, and baking powder; mix well. Stir in vanilla and eggs. Add pecans, if you choose, mixing well.

2) Pour into pie shell, and bake in preheated 350° oven 45 minutes or until set.

3) For Caramel Pecan Sauce, boil sugar and water in saucepan, stirring constantly. Add light and dark corn syrups; bring back to a boil, stirring constantly.

4) Stir in pecans, then remove from heat. Stir in vanilla, mixing well. (Can store in sealed quart jar in refrigerator until needed.) Stir well before serving.

Southern Praline Pie
with Caramel Pecan Sauce

189

CARAMEL CREAM PIE

SERVES 6–8.

The recipe was given to Mama in the 60's and became a favorite on The Crown's dessert cart. She made two at a time, once or twice a week, and there was never any left at the end of lunch! This is a southern "pass-along recipe" that I hope you'll enjoy with your family, and pass it along to your friends.

1¾ cups sugar, divided

3 rounded tablespoons cornstarch

1½ cups milk

½ teaspoon vanilla

4 eggs, separated

3 tablespoons unsalted butter

1 (9-inch) pie shell, baked

1) In a large saucepan, combine ¾ cup sugar, cornstarch, milk, and butter, and cook on medium heat, stirring constantly, until custard begins to thicken.

2) Beat egg yolks with a fork. Add a spoon of hot custard to yolks, and blend to warm yolks. Add 2–3 more spoonfuls of custard, then slowly add yolk mixture and vanilla into custard, stirring well. Cook until very thick. Remove from heat, but keep warm.

3) Immediately place a skillet on medium-hot eye, and sprinkle ½ cup sugar in skillet. Watch carefully as sugar begins to brown deeply and bubble; do not stir. When sugar is melted, pour caramelized sugar into hot custard, and mix completely. Pour into baked pie shell.

4) Beat egg whites on high. When soft peaks form, sprinkle with remaining ½ cup sugar, and beat until stiff peaks form.

5) Spread meringue to edge to seal. Place pie in preheated 350° oven, and bake about 10 minutes, until meringue is nicely browned. Cool before slicing.

PIES

CREAMY PEANUT BUTTER PIE

SERVES 6–8.

This creamy custard pie has always been popular in the Delta. It is just simply delicious! Peanut butter is one of my comfort foods, and this pie is the ultimate!

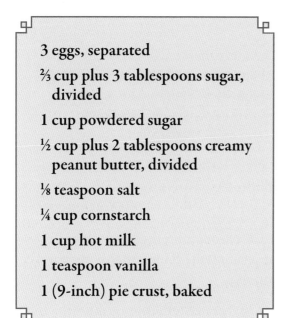

3 eggs, separated

⅔ cup plus 3 tablespoons sugar, divided

1 cup powdered sugar

½ cup plus 2 tablespoons creamy peanut butter, divided

⅛ teaspoon salt

¼ cup cornstarch

1 cup hot milk

1 teaspoon vanilla

1 (9-inch) pie crust, baked

1) Beat egg whites until soft peaks form; slowly add 3 tablespoons sugar, and beat until meringue is stiff. Set aside.

2) Combine powdered sugar and ½ cup peanut butter in small bowl, and blend until crumbly. Set aside.

3) In heavy saucepan (not on stove), beat egg yolks, then add remaining ⅔ cup sugar, salt, and cornstarch. Gradually add hot milk, beating well. Set saucepan on low heat, stirring constantly, until mixture is thick, about 10 minutes. Take off heat, add remaining 2 tablespoons peanut butter and vanilla, and continue stirring until mixture is cool.

4) Sprinkle all but 1 tablespoon peanut butter/sugar mixture into cooled pie crust. Pour custard on top, and smooth to edges.

5) Spread meringue on custard, taking right to the edge, sealing the custard. Sprinkle remaining 1 tablespoon peanut butter/ sugar mixture on top of meringue.

6) Bake in preheated 350° oven until meringue is lightly browned, about 10 minutes. Cool completely, then refrigerate.

Aunt Doris's Chocolate Pie

SERVES 6–8.

The trouble with this pie is, it's so good you just can't stop eating it! This recipe was a specialty of Aunt Doris, who gave the recipe to our niece Katie, who keeps the tradition of her chocolate pie alive in the family. That's what southerners do—we make food memories.

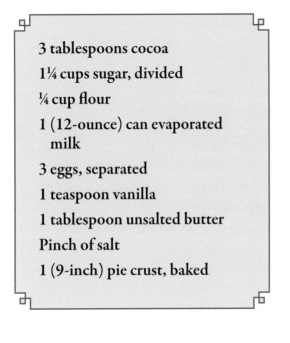

3 tablespoons cocoa

1¼ cups sugar, divided

¼ cup flour

1 (12-ounce) can evaporated milk

3 eggs, separated

1 teaspoon vanilla

1 tablespoon unsalted butter

Pinch of salt

1 (9-inch) pie crust, baked

1) In a saucepan, place cocoa, 1 cup sugar, and flour; mix well. Stir in just enough evaporated milk to make a paste, dissolving cocoa, sugar, and flour.

2) Beat egg yolks, add to chocolate mixture, and beat well. Add remaining evaporated milk, and cook over medium heat, stirring constantly, until mixture thickens.

3) Remove from heat, then mix in vanilla, butter, and salt. Pour custard into baked pie crust.

4) Beat egg whites until soft peaks form, then slowly add remaining ¼ cup sugar until stiff peaks form.

5) Spread meringue over custard, and brown in preheated 350° oven until lightly browned.

PIES

MISSISSIPPI DELTA FUDGE PIE

SERVES 6–8.

One of Mama's friends made this pie when I was in elementary school, and I loved it. She gave Mama the recipe, and Mama gave it to me when I married. We both made it for years, but not always in a pie shell—and that was the joy of it! All chocolate, and so deeply rich and gooey! When we opened The Crown, I named it Mississippi Delta Fudge Pie, baked it in a pie shell, and it became the favorite of every little boy and girl who ate lunch with us! And it still is!

1 stick unsalted butter

4 tablespoons cocoa

1¾ cups granulated sugar

¼ cup all-purpose flour

1 teaspoon vanilla

4 eggs, beaten

1 (9-inch) pie crust, unbaked (optional)

1) Melt butter in saucepan or microwave. Add cocoa, and stir well.

2) Add sugar, flour, vanilla, and eggs, stirring to combine thoroughly.

3) Pour into pie crust (or buttered pie pan), and bake in preheated 350° oven 40–45 minutes.

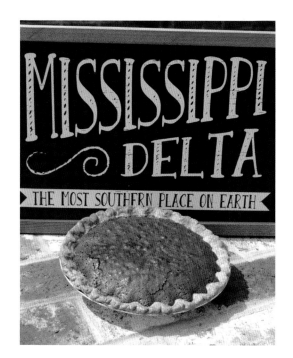

193

BRANDY ALEXANDER PIE

SERVES 6–8.

When Mama was making this pie for her bridge parties and club meetings, she had to make the cookie crust from scratch. These days, you can buy this type of crust, but I still like to make my own when time allows. It's a great pie to make days ahead, and freeze. Wonderfully light to serve after a heavy dinner.

½ stick butter, melted

1½ cups chocolate cookie crumbs (Mama used Oreos)

3 cups miniature marshmallows (or 32 large ones)

½ cup milk

¼ cup crème de cacao or Kahlúa

3 tablespoons brandy

1½ cups whipping cream, whipped

Milk chocolate candy bar, to grate as garnish

1) Melt butter in bowl or saucepan. Add cookie crumbs, and mix well. Press mixture into bottom and up side of a glass pie pan.

2) Bake in preheated 350° oven 10 minutes. Cool. (Or buy a prepared chocolate crumb crust.)

3) Combine marshmallows and milk in saucepan; cook over low heat, stirring constantly, until marshmallows have melted.

4) Cool, then add crème de cacao and brandy, mixing well. Fold this mixture into the whipped cream. Pour combined mixture into pie shell, and chill in refrigerator.

5) When ready to serve, grate chocolate in large ribbons over pie to garnish. Refrigerate until ready to cut and serve. (Pie freezes well; just thaw for several hours before serving.)

OTHER DESSERTS

Mississippi Peach Cobbler

MISSISSIPPI PEACH COBBLER

SERVES 6–8.

As she got older, my grandmother Momo made peach cobbler every Sunday instead of a pie, and she didn't mind a bit using a big can of peaches instead of fresh fruit. It can be either, but I promise that a big can of peaches makes a mighty good cobbler.

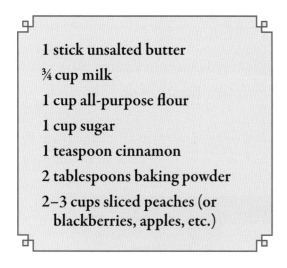

1 stick unsalted butter

¾ cup milk

1 cup all-purpose flour

1 cup sugar

1 teaspoon cinnamon

2 tablespoons baking powder

2–3 cups sliced peaches (or blackberries, apples, etc.)

1) Place butter in 9x13-inch baking dish. Put dish in 350° oven to melt butter.

2) In large bowl, combine milk, flour, sugar, cinnamon, and baking powder, mixing well. Pour batter in center of melted butter, but do not stir.

3) Add peaches all over batter, but do not stir.

4) Bake in hot oven until crust is golden brown, 35–40 minutes.

TIDBIT: The eight-foot hedge around our house in England was smothered in blackberries. Momo visited twice during the season, and made some incredible cobblers for us.

DELICIOUS DESSERT CRÊPES

SERVES 10–12.

Crêpes always look so elegant on the plate. Use strawberries, raspberries, blueberries, fresh peaches, or whatever is in season. Frozen fruit works well, but fresh is always a plus. Make your own crêpes (page 43) or purchase packaged crêpes.

DESSERT CRÊPE FILLING:

2 (8-ounce) packages cream cheese, at room temperature

4 tablespoons sour cream

1 teaspoon vanilla

1 (1-pound) box confectioners' sugar

FRUIT SAUCE:

1 cup fresh orange juice, divided

1½ tablespoons cornstarch

½ cup packed brown sugar

1–2 tablespoons freshly grated orange rind

2–3 cups sliced strawberries, whole raspberries, blueberries, etc.

2 tablespoons Grand Marnier (optional)

1) In a bowl, mix cream cheese, sour cream, and vanilla; beat until smooth. Add sugar and continue to beat until firm. (Can refrigerate filling at this point. Filling holds well for a week.)

2) Place 1–2 tablespoons filling down center of each crêpe. Fold one end over filling and pull slightly to tighten filling, then roll each crêpe into a cylinder. Stack in pan, and refrigerate until ready to serve.

3) For Fruit Sauce, combine 3 tablespoons orange juice with cornstarch; set aside.

4) In large saucepan on medium heat, mix remaining orange juice and sugar until dissolved. Add cornstarch mixture, and stir until it begins to thicken. Add orange rind and strawberries (or your choice of fruit), stirring vigorously until well mixed.

5) Set sauce aside until ready to serve over crêpes. Sauce will hold refrigerated for 2 days. Add Grand Marnier, if you desire, just before serving.

6) To serve, place two filled crêpes on each dessert plate. Spoon sauce across crêpes.

THE CROWN'S PAVLOVA

SERVES 8.

We've served Pavlova at The Crown—always on a cake stand—since we opened in 1976. It has always been a favorite, because this beautiful dessert is so light and airy, just like the Russian ballerina who danced in New Zealand and Australia in the 1900's. Both countries claim creating this fabulous dessert in her honor. I'm forever grateful to my dear Scottish friend, Joan Mangnall, for giving me this authentic recipe by her Australian cousin!

2 teaspoons cornstarch

1 cup granulated sugar

3 egg whites

1 teaspoon vinegar

8 ounces heavy cream, whipped, or Cool Whip

1 cup sliced fresh fruit (strawberries, raspberries, kiwi, peaches, or apricots)

2 tablespoons toasted almonds or pecans to garnish

1) Preheat oven to 325°. Heavily butter a metal or glass pie pan.

2) Mix cornstarch and sugar in a small bowl, and set aside.

3) Beat egg whites with an electric mixer until soft peaks form. Slowly sprinkle sugar/cornstarch mixture into egg whites while continuing to beat. When stiff peaks form, sprinkle vinegar directly over meringue, and beat slowly to mix in well.

4) Place meringue in pie pan, spreading evenly to edge. Bake 35 minutes, then reduce heat to 200° for another 30 minutes. The Pavlova shell will be very lightly browned, and will probably sink in and crack when removed from oven. Shell will store, lightly covered, for 2 days. Fill Pavlova just before you are ready to serve.

5) For filling, mix whipped cream with fresh fruit, and spoon onto shell. Spread evenly almost to the edge of shell, like filling in a pie crust. Garnish with toasted almonds. (Pavlova is gluten free, and can be made with Cool Whip—and that is a plus for many people.)

TIP: Individual bite-size Pavlova make a wonderful pick-up dessert. Prepare Pavlova as usual, then drop a tablespoon onto parchment paper. With back of spoon, make a little dent in the meringue, so the filling has a place to rest. Bake about 10 minutes, until lightly browned, then lower oven temp to 200° and bake another 10–15 minutes. Watch carefully because cooking time depends on size.

The Crown's Pavlova

CREAMY BANANA PUDDING

SERVE 10–12.

This quick banana pudding gets raves from everyone who eats it, and there's never a bite left in the bowl. I love the meringue on the old-fashioned puddings, but this version is satisfying and delicious, with a fraction of the effort.

1½ cups milk

1 (14-ounce) can sweetened condensed milk

1 (3-ounce) package vanilla instant pudding mix

1 teaspoon vanilla

1 (16-ounce) tub Cool Whip, thawed

6–8 bananas

1 (11-ounce) box vanilla wafers

1) In a bowl, combine thoroughly the milk and sweetened condensed milk. Stir in pudding mix and vanilla until thoroughly mixed.

2) Place in refrigerator 5 minutes while pudding thickens. Fold Cool Whip into pudding, mixing well. (Save a scoop of Cool Whip for decoration, if desired.)

3) Spoon a layer of pudding into large serving bowl. Add a layer of sliced bananas, then a layer of vanilla wafers. Repeat layers 2 or 3 times, finishing with pudding on top. Refrigerate until ready to serve.

Old-Fashioned Banana Pudding

SERVES 8–10.

Banana pudding was always on the sideboard at any gathering—family potlucks, community fish frys, dinners on the grounds at church—or when we asked Mama for it! I love that meringue sitting on top of the pudding, and though it does refrigerate, it seldom lasts that long.

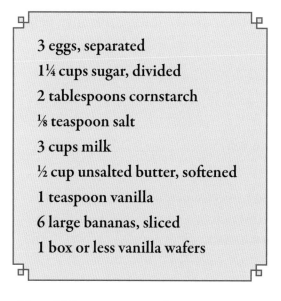

3 eggs, separated

1¼ cups sugar, divided

2 tablespoons cornstarch

⅛ teaspoon salt

3 cups milk

½ cup unsalted butter, softened

1 teaspoon vanilla

6 large bananas, sliced

1 box or less vanilla wafers

TIP: I like very creamy banana pudding, so I use fewer vanilla wafers, one-third to one-half less. If I'm making it for Prescott, I add more wafers...make every recipe your own.

1) Beat egg yolks with fork, and set aside. Beat egg whites with electric mixer until soft peaks form; slowly add ¼ cup sugar, and beat until meringue is stiff; set aside.

2) Mix remaining 1 cup sugar, cornstarch, and salt in large saucepan. Over medium heat, slowly add milk, stirring constantly, while custard cooks. When custard is beginning to thicken, take 3 spoons of hot custard (1 spoon at a time) and beat into bowl of egg yolks to warm yolks. Mix well, then very slowly drizzle egg mixture into custard, stirring well and constantly until custard is thick. Remove from heat.

3) Add butter in pieces to custard with vanilla, stirring vigorously until mixed well. Cool custard slightly.

4) Layer bananas, vanilla wafers, and custard in buttered 2-quart baking dish in 3 layers. Spread meringue over last layer of custard to edge of dish. Bake in preheated 350° oven until meringue is golden.

The Crown's Bread Pudding

SERVES 8–10.

I have a weakness for bread pudding. Once, we spent five days in New Orleans, and ate bread pudding at every meal on a quest to find the best. This is the winner, with Lemon Sauce or Bourbon Sauce (page 217).

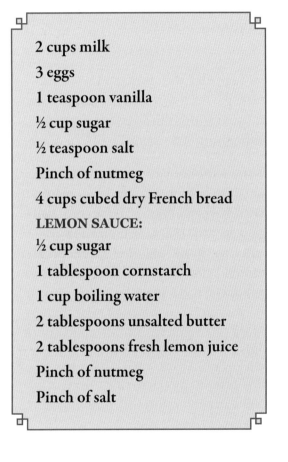

2 cups milk

3 eggs

1 teaspoon vanilla

½ cup sugar

½ teaspoon salt

Pinch of nutmeg

4 cups cubed dry French bread

LEMON SAUCE:

½ cup sugar

1 tablespoon cornstarch

1 cup boiling water

2 tablespoons unsalted butter

2 tablespoons fresh lemon juice

Pinch of nutmeg

Pinch of salt

1) In a large bowl, beat together milk, eggs, vanilla, sugar, salt, and nutmeg.

2) Fold bread gently into egg mixture. Pour into buttered 9x13-inch baking dish.

3) Bake in preheated 375° oven until raised and browned, about 40 minutes.

4) Serve warm with Lemon Sauce or Bourbon Sauce (page 217) or just plain, without sauce.

5) For Lemon Sauce, combine sugar and cornstarch in a saucepan. Gradually add water, and cook over medium heat until mixture is clear, stirring constantly 2–3 minutes.

6) Remove from heat, add butter, lemon juice, nutmeg, and salt, and stir well. Serve warm over warm bread pudding.

Chocolate Bread Pudding

SERVES 8–10.

This is not your usual bread pudding with chocolate thrown in. It is a treasure of its own—rich, creamy, and deeply chocolate.

4 squares baking chocolate

4 cups milk

5 eggs, separated

1 cup sugar

½ cup melted unsalted butter

1 teaspoon vanilla

2 cups fresh bread crumbs

Whipped cream to garnish

Dusting of cocoa to garnish

1) Cut chocolate squares into pieces. In large saucepan, on medium heat, place milk and chocolate, stirring until chocolate is melted. Set aside.

2) With electric mixer, beat egg whites until stiff, then transfer beaten whites to another bowl.

3) In same mixer bowl, beat egg yolks, adding sugar a little at a time. Add chocolate mixture, melted butter, and vanilla, and beat well. Transfer mixture to a large bowl. Fold bread crumbs into chocolate mixture, then gently fold in egg whites to combine well.

4) Pour mixture into well-buttered 9x13-inch baking dish. Bake in preheated 325° oven about 1 hour or until set. Insert sharp knife into pudding to check. Serve warm with whipped cream, and a dusting of cocoa to garnish.

THE CROWN'S SHERRY TRIFLE

SERVES 15–20.

Traditionally a beautiful Sunday dessert at homes in England, this was always a great treat when we were living there. Rather like a banana pudding with the custard, but so much more sophisticated in flavor with the cake and sherry. (Sometimes I get heavy handed with the sherry, and my customers at The Crown love that!)

1 (18¼-ounce) box yellow or white cake mix

⅔ cup cornstarch

⅔ cup sugar

5 cups milk

1½ teaspoons vanilla

2 cups chopped fruit (we use diced peaches at The Crown)

¼ cup or more sherry, sweet or dry

1 cup whipping cream, whipped, or Cool Whip

Toasted slivered almonds for garnish

TIP: Trifle can be made with a variety of fresh or canned fruit: strawberries, raspberries, peaches, apricots, whatever you choose. I don't use frozen fruit, because of the extra liquid.

1) Prepare cake mix according to directions on box, and bake in 9x13-inch pan.

2) Mix cornstarch and sugar in saucepan. Add milk, and place on medium heat, stirring constantly until thickened.

3) Take off heat, add vanilla, and stir well. Set aside to be used while warm.

4) Cut baked cake into 3 pieces. Place 1 piece in bottom of trifle bowl. Cut second piece into smaller pieces, using half to "fill in the gaps" around first piece.

5) Layer 1 cup fruit on cake, and sprinkle with half the sherry. Spoon half the custard on top.

6) Place third piece of cake on top of custard, and fill in gaps with remaining cake pieces. Repeat layering fruit, sherry, and custard. Cover with plastic wrap, and refrigerate until ready to serve. Trifle can be made 2–3 days ahead.

7) When ready to serve, cover top of trifle with whipped cream, and garnish with almonds.

The Crown's Sherry Trifle

FIT FOR A KING
CHOCOLATE ALMOND MOUSSE

SERVES 15–20.

Rich chocolate mousse on a nutty crust, with a sweet tart topping—great for a crowd!

1 cup all-purpose flour

¼ cup packed brown sugar

1½ sticks unsalted butter, divided

2 cups toasted sliced almonds, chopped, divided

2 envelopes unflavored gelatin

1½ cups milk, divided

1½ cups sugar

¼ teaspoon salt

2 egg yolks

¾ cup cocoa

1 cup whipping cream, whipped

1 cup sour cream

1 cup powdered sugar

1) Combine flour and brown sugar. Add ½ stick butter in small pieces; combine with fingers until crumbly. Pat firmly into lightly buttered 9x13-inch pan.

2) Bake at 350° for 12–15 minutes; do not brown. Sprinkle 1 cup almonds over crust, and set aside to cool.

3) Sprinkle gelatin over ½ cup milk in bowl to soften.

4) In saucepan, mix sugar, salt, egg yolks, cocoa, and remaining 1 stick butter. Add in remaining 1 cup milk, and cook over medium heat until well blended, stirring constantly.

5) Remove from heat; stir in softened gelatin. Return pan to heat, and stir until gelatin is dissolved. Chill until mixture begins to thicken, about 45 minutes.

6) Fold in whipped cream, and pour into prepared crust. Cover, and chill until firm, or overnight.

7) Mix sour cream and powdered sugar until smooth. Spread over mousse, and sprinkle remaining 1 cup almonds over top. Will hold refrigerated for several days.

HEAVENLY CRÈME BRÛLÉE

SERVES 4.

Crème brûlée is my absolute favorite dessert. Always my choice when I see it on a restaurant menu, and one I love to serve at home. This recipe is heavenly—and it's easy!

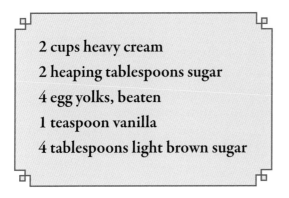

2 cups heavy cream

2 heaping tablespoons sugar

4 egg yolks, beaten

1 teaspoon vanilla

4 tablespoons light brown sugar

1) Heat cream in a boiler on medium heat, stirring until nicely hot, but not scalded. Stir in sugar until dissolved; remove from heat.

2) Beat egg yolks with a fork, and add to hot mixture, stirring well. Add vanilla, and stir until mixed. Pour into very lightly buttered individual shallow baking dishes.

3) Place dishes in a pan with enough warm water to come halfway up side of dishes. Carefully slide pan into a preheated 300° oven, and bake about 50 minutes. A knife should come out clean when stuck in center. Cool, and refrigerate until ready to serve. Overnight is fine.

4) When ready to serve, sprinkle top of each custard with brown sugar. Place electric oven rack on highest notch, and turn on broiler. When broiler is hot, put dishes on a cookie sheet, and place under broiler. Leave door open, and watch carefully. When sugar starts to melt, remove from broiler, and serve each dish immediately on a dessert plate.

CHERRIES JUBILEE

SERVES 4.

I love to serve Cherries Jubilee or Bananas Foster for special occasions. It's so deliciously simple to make but so elegantly impressive. Especially when Tony serves it flaming.

1 (16-ounce) can sweet dark cherries

1 tablespoon cornstarch

¼ cup currant jelly or grape preserves

1 teaspoon freshly squeezed lemon juice

⅓ cup brandy

Vanilla ice cream

1) Drain cherries, reserving syrup.

2) In a medium saucepan, combine reserved syrup, cornstarch, jelly, and lemon juice; mix well. Cook over low heat, stirring constantly, until thickened.

3) Add drained cherries, continuing to stir until warm and bubbly.

4) If you do not want to flame the sauce, add brandy; stir gently to combine and serve warm over ice cream.

5) If you do want the excitement of the flaming, pour brandy evenly over the warm bubbly sauce; avert your face, and ignite brandy with a long, lighted match, then shake the pan gently. Spoon flaming sauce with long-handled spoon over ice cream, or wait until flames have subsided to serve. (Waiting is less exciting but much safer, and the flavor is just as delicious!)

Harry Belafonte with Jennifer, Evelyn, and Tony, having dinner at The Crown when he and Sidney Poitier were in Indianola in the 90's promoting The Algebra Project in public schools.

SAUCES & SEASONINGS

The Crown's Sassy Seasoning

COMEBACK SAUCE

MAKES 1½ CUPS.

Recipe doubles or triples easily, so make a big batch and you'll always have some when you want to add a little kick to a sandwich (or pizzazz to your salad). Comeback is popular as a salad dressing at The Crown, and is wonderful as a dip for fresh vegetables, or just plain old crackers. It's a real Mississippi Delta thing!

1 cup mayonnaise

3 tablespoons grated onion

¼ cup chili sauce

½ cup ketchup

¼ cup pickle relish

1 tablespoon Worcestershire

1 teaspoon prepared mustard

1 teaspoon coarsely ground
   black pepper

1 teaspoon Tabasco

1 teaspoon garlic powder

1) In a medium bowl, thoroughly combine mayonnaise and onion.

2) Add remaining ingredients, and mix thoroughly.

3) Store in covered jar or container, refrigerated.

4) Serve as a dip, on salads, or as a sandwich spread.

JEZEBEL SAUCE

MAKES 1 QUART.

Jezebel is a traditional sauce our grandmothers and great-grandmothers always made at Thanksgiving and Christmas to serve with ham. The holidays are a good time to serve it, but Jezebel Sauce deserves to be enjoyed year-round. It's wonderful just poured over cream cheese and served with crackers. Broiled chicken or fish get a boost of flavor with just a dab of Jezebel. It's fabulous as a dipping sauce for boiled shrimp or fried shrimp. Sliced ham and turkey sandwiches also like Jezebel Sauce for that extra jazz-up!

SAUCES

1 (18-ounce) jar peach preserves

1 (18-ounce) jar apple jelly

1 (5-ounce) jar horseradish

1 (1.75-ounce) can dry mustard

2 tablespoons coarsely ground black pepper

1) Cook preserves and jelly in large saucepan over medium heat, stirring, until melted together. Remove from heat.

2) Add horseradish, mustard, and black pepper, stirring to blend thoroughly.

3) Pour into jars, and refrigerate. Jezebel Sauce will keep in the refrigerator indefinitely.

TIDBIT: Jezebel Sauce is served at The Crown with our Royal Sandwich—roast beef and Swiss cheese toasted on French bread. I like it so much that I smear it all over the sandwich, and then dip it in what's left in the sauce cup. It makes great gifts in cute jars, so there is no excuse for not enjoying one of the South's greatest sauces!

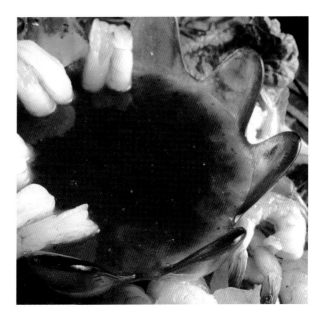

YOGURT LEMON SAUCE

MAKES 1 CUP.

This deliciously healthy sauce makes a simple baked fish or chicken breast taste extra special. It's also delicious as a dipping sauce for fresh vegetables.

1 cup plain yogurt

1 clove garlic, minced

Juice of 1 lemon

1 green onion, finely sliced

1 teaspoon dried dill weed

½ teaspoon white pepper

¼ teaspoon salt

1) In a glass bowl, mix all ingredients well.

2) Refrigerate for several hours before using. Sauce will hold well for 2–3 days.

PLUM SAUCE

MAKES 2 CUPS.

Plum Sauce is delicious as a dipping sauce for fried fish or chicken. Drizzle it over grilled or broiled meats that need an extra kick of flavor. Pour a little over a block of cream cheese as an appetizer with crackers.

1½ cups red plum jam

1½ tablespoons prepared mustard

1½ tablespoons prepared horseradish

1½ teaspoons fresh lemon juice

1) In a small saucepan on medium heat, mix all ingredients.

2) Stir until jam is melted, and sauce is blended.

3) Serve immediately, or cool to room temperature. Store refrigerated indefinitely.

GREEK CUCUMBER SAUCE

MAKES 2 CUPS.

This sauce is like Tzatziki sauce served on Greek sandwiches. Our cucumber sauce gives a fresh clean flavor to grilled fish or chicken. Especially delicious drizzled over grilled meats served over rice. I like to serve it on freshly sliced tomatoes...and cucumbers... and green salads...and fish sandwiches.... Use your imagination, and enjoy!

1 small cucumber, grated (do not peel)

1 clove garlic, minced

1 cup plain yogurt

1 teaspoon fresh lemon juice

1 tablespoon chopped fresh mint or dill

1 green onion, minced

1) Grate cucumber into a small bowl.

2) Add garlic, yogurt, lemon juice, mint, and onion, and mix well. Taste, and add salt only if needed.

3) Refrigerates well for up to 3 days.

SAUCES

213

SIMPLE HOLLANDAISE SAUCE

MAKES 1 CUP.

This sauce will double with good results. I always double it, because I love having this great sauce in the refrigerator ready to enjoy when I need it. It will keep about a week, but another great meal with it should never be more than a week away!

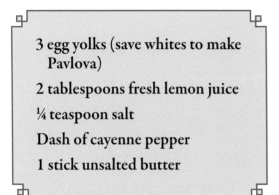

3 egg yolks (save whites to make Pavlova)

2 tablespoons fresh lemon juice

¼ teaspoon salt

Dash of cayenne pepper

1 stick unsalted butter

TIDBIT: Hollandaise is a part of The Crown's Catfish Royale recipe, but is also wonderful used to dress fresh asparagus or broccoli. Serve over poached eggs sitting on a slice of ham on a toasted English Muffin, and you have Eggs Benedict, or Eggs Sardou on an artichoke heart. Dream up your own combination using the Hollandaise—it makes a special breakfast fabulous.

1) Place yolks, lemon juice, salt, and cayenne in blender.

2) Break butter into pieces, place in small saucepan, and heat until bubbling.

3) Cover blender, and blend egg yolk mixture at top speed for 2 seconds. Uncover, and still blending at top speed, pour in hot butter in a thin stream. (Use towel, if necessary, to protect from splashes.) Taste sauce, and add more seasoning, if needed.

4) Use sauce immediately, or pour into a container, and place in a bowl of lukewarm water to keep warm. The sauce can be refrigerated, brought to room temperature, and then slowly brought to a pouring consistency in a bath of slightly warm water, stirring carefully.

BLACK BUTTER

MAKES ½ CUP.

We first tasted this flavorful Black Butter in a small hotel on the coast of France in 1972. We were the first guests of the season, so we spent many lovely hours visiting with the owner, talking food, and cooking. We loved the Black Butter so much, we experimented with lots of other ways to enjoy it. Now we use it to flavor cooked asparagus, green beans, catfish, and sautéed chicken breasts.

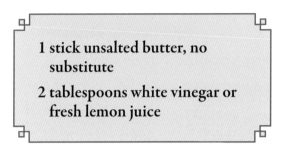

1 stick unsalted butter, no substitute

2 tablespoons white vinegar or fresh lemon juice

TIP: It's nice to keep a tub of Black Butter ready for whenever you need it. Black butter will keep for weeks in the refrigerator to be used later on beans, asparagus, or broccoli. The trick is to drain the cooked vegetables well, so the butter clings to the hot vegetables. At The Crown, we brown at least two pounds of butter at a time!

1) Put butter in a stainless pan, so you can see color of butter as it browns.

2) Melt butter, and continue to cook over medium heat; watch as it turns to a rich, nutty brown, then nearly black.

3) When butter has ALMOST burned, take pan off heat; step back, and slowly add vinegar at arm's length; it will foam and splatter on you if you are too close, so be careful. Stir, and set aside until needed.

4) The butter is finished at this point. Use immediately, or cool and keep refrigerated until needed.

Larry's BBQ Sauce

MAKES 9 CUPS.

My brother-in-law, Larry Adams and his brother Harry are truly dedicated to the art of grilling and BBQ. Their team, called Adams' Ribs, won second place at the Blues, Bikes and BBQ contest during the B. B. King Homecoming Festival in 2011 with this sauce recipe—and their luscious ribs.

½ cup chopped onion

3 tablespoons oil

1 (64-ounce) bottle ketchup

2 tablespoons soy sauce

2 tablespoons teriyaki sauce

2 tablespoons Worcestershire

2 tablespoons Louisiana Hot Sauce

4 tablespoons prepared mustard

¾ cup packed brown sugar

1) In a large pot, cook onion with oil 3–4 minutes.

2) Add remaining ingredients, stir thoroughly, and simmer 30–45 minutes.

3) Cool, and put into jars to store in refrigerator.

4) To use, baste on chicken, ribs, Boston butt, beef, and also offer for dipping and drizzling at the table.

THE CROWN'S BOURBON SAUCE

MAKES 3½ CUPS.

The bridge players at The Crown request bread pudding often—and usually with bourbon sauce! That's the way I like it, too—and I'm passionate about bread pudding.

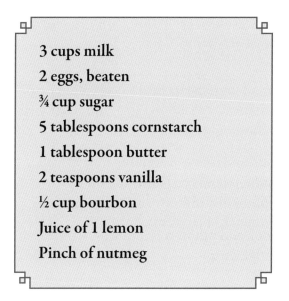

3 cups milk

2 eggs, beaten

¾ cup sugar

5 tablespoons cornstarch

1 tablespoon butter

2 teaspoons vanilla

½ cup bourbon

Juice of 1 lemon

Pinch of nutmeg

1) Bring milk to a boil in small saucepan.

2) In another saucepan, mix eggs, sugar, cornstarch, and butter. Pour hot milk into egg mixture, stirring vigorously, and cook on low heat until sauce thickens, stirring constantly.

3) When sauce is thick, remove from heat; add vanilla, bourbon, lemon juice, and nutmeg, stirring to blend completely.

4) Serve warm over The Crown's Bread Pudding (page 202) or vanilla ice cream.

TIP: Bourbon sauce can be refrigerated for several days. Just warm gently, adding a little milk, if needed, to make it smooth.

SAUCES

THE CROWN'S SASSY SEASONING

MAKES ABOUT 3 CUPS.

Sassy is the "secret ingredient" in a lot of my dishes. We sprinkle a little Sassy on chicken breasts, pork, beef, and vegetables before roasting or grilling. Anytime I want a peppery flavor, I reach for Sassy. You only need a little bit to get lots of flavor.

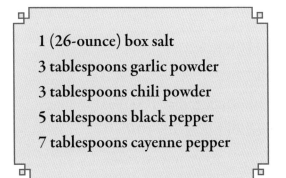

1 (26-ounce) box salt
3 tablespoons garlic powder
3 tablespoons chili powder
5 tablespoons black pepper
7 tablespoons cayenne pepper

1) Put all ingredients into a half-gallon jar or container. Put lid on tight, and shake well to thoroughly mix.

2) Pour some Sassy Seasoning into a smaller shaker jar to keep handy in your spice cupboard, and store the rest in a sealed container or jar, ready for refills.

Hambone loves greeting guests at The Crown. If he doesn't already know you, you'll be friends before you leave.

INDEX

INDEX

INDEX

INDEX

ABOUT THE AUTHOR

Evelyn Roughton is the chief cook and creator of all things yummy at The Crown, Indianola, Mississippi's famous and beloved landmark. The Crown opened as an English antique shop in 1972, and now it's an art gallery, gift shop, bookstore, gourmet food shop, AND a restaurant.

The Crown began serving lunch in the antique shop with a pub setting almost 40 years ago, in March of 1976—out in the cotton fields north of Indianola.

Evelyn is a lover and promoter of all things delicious, and all things Mississippi, especially the Mississippi Delta. She enjoys good food, spending time with her precious family, and talking to visitors at The Crown, directing them to the Blues heritage sites, the B.B. King Museum, and all the wonderful out-of-the-way places to visit in the Delta.

Evelyn is very active in the Indianola community. She is involved in the Indianola Chamber Main Street, B.B. King Museum, Indianola Garden Club, Indianola Civic League, and Indian Bayou Arts Festival. She has been the recipient of the Indianola Citizen of the Year award, the Delta Council Good Middling Lady Award, and the Indianola Blues Society Promotions Award. Evelyn is a member and Sunday School teacher at First United Methodist Church.

Evelyn graduated from Troy University in 1964, and soon after married Tony Roughton. The two traveled extensively while Tony was in the Air Force. They are the parents of two children: Jennifer Schaumburg runs the Crown, often with help from her two children, Sage and Prescott; and Kevin Roughton who lives in Maine with his wife Deanna Contrino and with their two children, Izabela and Carter.

Carter, Kevin, Izabela, Deanna, Tony, Evelyn, Jennifer, Prescott, and Sage on a family vacation.